MAGGIE'S REVENGE

First Edition

By

Dr. Hollis A. Palmer

**Deep Roots Publications,
Saratoga Springs, N. Y.**

Maggie's Revenge

By Hollis A. Palmer

Published by:
Deep Roots Publications
P. O. Box 114
Saratoga Springs, NY 12866

Printed in the United States of America

First Printing September 2001

Library of Congress Cataloging-in-Publication Data
Palmer, Dr. Hollis A. 1946 -
Maggie's Revenge
Includes Index
ISBN 0-9671713-9-3
Library of Congress Catalog Card Number
2001118691

This book is dedicated to my father

Lawrence Palmer

who has demonstrated once again
that he has a will of iron.

And to

The memory of

Maggie Horrigan

may her story live on.

Special Thanks to

Nicole Stein

who for a second time has struggled with my thoughts

And

Jim Russo

Of The Graphic Zone for
his creative contributions

And the staff of the following institutions
for helping with my search

The Greenwich Library
The Fort Edward Historical Society
The Greenwich Historian
The Washington County Historian
The Crandall Library- Glens Falls
The Troy Public Library
The Albany Public Library

Maggie's Revenge

Acknowledgements

One of the most common questions asked when doing presentations is why I get involved in the protracted research required for each of the various true crime cases. Having published *Crimes in Time Journal*, and individual stories like *To Spend Eternity Alone* occasionally, and only occasionally, is there an atrocity to which this author becomes mysteriously drawn and compelled to investigate until all apparent resources are exhausted. This is the situation in the case of the murder of the young household maid, Maggie Horrigan.

I became aware of the Horrigan murder after doing a presentation for the book *To Spend Eternity Alone*. One of the historians, who invited me to speak knew of the Hill Collection at Adirondack Community College. He suggested that I look at the research of William Hill who had been deeply interested in the Billings murder and the murder of "some maid."

William Hill and I do not agree on the perpetrator in the Billings case or on some of the points and people in the Horrigan case. In examining Hill's work beyond Billings, my eyes were opened to the Horrigan case and the probable parties guilty of Maggie's death. Although I don't agree with all of his logic, for his efforts I will be forever grateful.

William Hart Hill

William Hart Hill was a native of Fort Edward who, in addition to being a successful businessman and politician, was also an historian. Born in 1891, two years after the murder of Maggie Horrigan, Hill attended school in Fort Edward and Glens Falls. In addition to his retail hardware business, Mr. Hill ran the Newton and Hill Explosives Company and was president of the Fort Edward National Bank prior to its merger with Glens Fall Bank and Trust. He also served as mayor of Fort Edward from 1923-1924.

Hill had an intense interest in local history and wrote several books and articles on Fort Edward and its vicinity. The Hill collection, at Adirondack Community College consists of over 1,000 books, scrapbooks and documents, which makes it one of the best resources in the area. The Hill collection should be visited by anyone that wants to gain an understanding of local history or who is interested in genealogy in this area.

Mr. Hill, may you rest knowing that through your efforts Maggie's struggle for justice has continued.

And to Maggie, may you now rest in peace knowing that many more, of yet another generation, will seek the answer to your mystery.

A GHOST STORY?

"My mother always told me the old stone bridge was haunted. It was probably just one of the stories parents tell their kids to keep them in line. I will admit, however, I always walked a little faster when I had to cross the bridge alone after dark."

Don McGrouty, age 73

Mr. Hill,
The attached is from the mother of my friend in Chicago.
I thought it might interest you.
K. Hubbard
She typed this mess. (Message) and then had a nightmare.

Unsigned note found
attached to a letter in
Hill's Horrigan file.

"Before I began the research on this book I never believed in ghosts. I never denied the power of the mind or the human spirit but rejected the idea of ghosts. Even now I am not sure that they exist. What I am sure of is that nothing else explains the ending of this true tale."

Hollis A. Palmer, Ph.D.

Table of Contents

Maps based on those from the 1866 Atlas of Washington County.

Map of site based on one originally designed by William Hill.

Photographs Courtesy of Fort Edward Historical Society.

June 1895

was a horrendously hot month in the industrial and transportation center of Fort Edward, New York. On June 18th during that period between late night and early morning, when truth and lies mingle in the deep shadows of darkness, a group of men were attempting to beat the oppressive heat of their rooms by sitting out on the porch of the Waverly House. The Waverly was a gentleman's boarding house located adjacent to the railroad tracks on South Broadway. The boarding house was typical of those of that period with a long open veranda that ran the entire front width of the building. The men who gathered that night all had rooms at one of the local boarding houses. Wisely, they had elected to leave the windows open so their rooms would cool while they sat out in the night air.

The men who gathered together that evening had known each other for years. Although occasionally participating in the rambling conversation, one lonely man was consumed in his own reflections. The lonely man's personal deliberations had nothing to do with the events of the day, the weather, or any other topics the group had spent the evening discussing.

For the lonely man, June had been a dire, vexing month. His best friend, who was only in his thirties, had died less than two weeks earlier. The death was attributed to an accidental drowning. He knew it was not that simple. He and the drowning victim had been friends since they were children. Common experiences in their youth had caused their lives to be permanently intertwined.

They had both married. They both had young children whom they doted over. They both were living apart from their wives. They both lived in boarding houses, although his friend could have lived better. Both had made mistakes in their lives. Substantial evidence we have today tells us that one of the mistakes they made, they made together.

1

The political and social contacts of the drowning victim's father made it inevitable that every paper in the county would carry the report of his death. As a true tribute to the father's power and influence the victim's obituary had taken over a full column in each of the area's newspapers.

Now, sitting on the boarding house porch with this group of men the lonely man realized he was truly isolated. Through his friend's death he had lost both his ally and the refuge of his friend's father's connections. The duplicity so carefully planned and followed for the previous five years had unraveled so quickly.

There had been two other deaths just two months earlier. The first April death had not been of a friend, but an associate. TB, the slow consumer of previously healthy victims, had struck this associate. Then came the rumors that the associate had made a confession on his deathbed. Foolishly, his friend's connected father had written a letter to the editor to each of the local newspapers, denying the gossip.

The unnecessary exposure brought on by the letter resulted in a second associate hanging himself less than three weeks later. The hanging victim's own young son had found him dangling from the rafters of his livery stable.

For some time, the drowning victim had suffered from anxiety, but the two April deaths and revival of the story seemed to push him over the edge. Drowning was the vehicle that finished the life that had ended some time before.

One of the men sitting on the porch that night would later tell an historian what transpired next, "As the train approached he arose, recited a verse of poetry and deliberately stepped in front of the sleeper." The lonely man was struck and thrown against a telegraph pole. His head was crushed.

To some, the railroad death was the last in a long-running set of tragedies. To many more, it brought to mind the truth of the expression "what tangled webs we weave". To even more, it was the fourth and final chapter of *Maggie's Revenge*.

Greenwich,

New York, embodies the deep rustic heritage of those harmonious New England villages whose quaint personalities were so skillfully captured by regional artist Grandma Moses. The Victorian houses have been so meticulously cared for throughout the years that even today the residences remain in a unique lived in, yet pristine condition. So uniform is the architectural tradition of the community that it takes virtually no imagination to picture the village a hundred years ago. Greenwich, after all, is one of those beautiful places where we all dream that we would like to live and raise a family. It is a place where the social order is well established and strictly adhered to. It is a village where the good side of town and the wrong side of the tracks are distinctly defined. Even more important to the social order is that in communities like Greenwich people from the different strata rarely cross paths.

Greenwich is a place where at night you can walk the streets without the fear that permeates the cities just a few hundred miles away. Of course, even the safest, most peaceful and wholesome village usually retains a regrettable moment that few want to remember.

Saturday morning, October 19, 1889,
was one of those moments for Greenwich.

At the time, the town's road crew still worked a half-day on Saturday mornings. On this particular Saturday, the town's workers were scheduled to repair the gravel highway between Middle Falls and Greenwich. The site where they were to work was near the stone bridge that passed over a small mill brook. Earlier in the century there had actually been a small mill just down stream from the bridge. The mill building was gone, but the foundation and dam that held the water for power still

3

remained. Downstream from this dam and still farther from the road was yet another dam that retained water for yet another mill. After the second mill, the water flowed a short distance into the Battenkill River.

Sixty-year-old Reuben Stewart was the foreman in charge of the crew that ominous morning. Stewart was also the president of the village legislature, a position politically equivalent to mayor of Greenwich – in short Stewart was a well connected person. Before going to the site where the men were to work, Stewart started his workday by picking up a wagonload of gravel to use in the repairs. He joined the rest of the men at the bridge about 8:00 a.m. When the first man arrived at the site around 7:00 a.m., he noticed a woman's hat and sacque (a style of shawl) resting on a fallen log near the road. The log was slightly northwest of the bridge, on the side of the brook closer to Middle Falls. Shortly after Stewart arrived he also noticed the neatly piled clothes. The men in the crew were basically honest and had left the items where they lay, assuming their owner would return at any moment to collect them.

When break time arrived at 9:00 a.m. no one had come for the clothes. Something about the clothes bothered Stewart so he decided to investigate. To get to the log Stewart had to climb over a fence and then go through approximately twenty-five feet of light brush. The shawl was neatly folded and on top of it was a blue straw hat with a hatpin through it. The hat was distinguished in that its owner had trimmed the hatband with white dove wings. Stewart thought it best to check the pockets of the shawl to see if there was anything that would help identify the owner. This was a good idea that unfortunately did not work since there were no pockets in the simple sacque. Unable to determine the owner, Stewart put the clothes down and went back up to the road.

Still curious about why the clothes were left out, Stewart walked to the bridge to look into the creek and the upper pond below. From his perch on the side of the bridge, Stewart was unable to see anything suspicious in the water below. With some trepidation he went back to work. Stewart tried to assure himself the clothes were a hoax.

Even after he returned the hat and shawl to the log there was something about the unclaimed clothes that continued to trouble Stewart.

After the break, Stewart accompanied the men while they went for a second load of gravel. Throughout the ride the clothes continued to bother Stewart. A little while after they arrived back at the site, he went back to the bridge and looked into the creek for a second time. Still unable to see anything of note he started down the slope to get a better view of the area. When he was part way down the steep embankment, at a point even with the first dam, he detected what he thought to be a dark shadow in the small lower millpond. The shadow was near the shore of the pond. The lower pond was long and narrow being only twenty feet across. Realizing Stewart had seen something amiss, two of the crewmembers joined him as he continued down to investigate. When they were farther down the bank Stewart and the other men were certain that what they had seen floating in the shallow water was the body of a young woman.

When the men

were finally able to reach the shore of the millpond, Stewart looked at his watch and noted the time was half past ten. The men saw the girl was floating face down in the shallow water, her long red hair spilling out about her head. The head and

5

shoulders of the lady were buoyant on the surface. The clothes were unruffled, with her skirt coming all the way down to her ankles. The head floated toward the bank and the legs were out toward the center of the small pond. There was no current in the small pond so the body had neither floated into its present location nor was it going to drift out.

The men estimated that the depth of the water where the upper body floated was eighteen inches (it would later be measured at twenty-three inches). Even that seemed cold and deep after the frost the previous evening, so the men did not want to wade into the water. Stewart had John Dwyer, one of the other men who had come down the bank, hand him a rock to put in the water. Stewart wanted to stand on it so he could get closer to the corpse, without getting his feet wet. He placed the large rock in the shallow water between the bank and the body. Then Stewart cautiously stepped onto the rock. Still unable to reach the torso, he pulled on the loose hair until the body moved closer to the shore. Stewart gently turned the body over and saw that the eyes and mouth were closed and the hands were clasped together in front of the girl's torso. The beautiful long hair was loose so the action of turning the body over caused strands to cover the girl's face. Tenderly, Stewart brushed the hair from the face and noticed it was a very pretty young woman whom he judged to be twenty years old. The eyes and mouth were both closed tightly, so tight that it appeared the lips had been bitten. Certain the woman was beyond help, Stewart turned the woman's body back over, preparing to leave the corpse in the water roughly as he had found it. Later, Stewart had been unable to say if the hands were touching the bottom of the shallow pond, although he suspected they were not in contact with the stony bottom. He would also later state that he did not believe the feet had been touching the bottom when he first came upon the body. Stewart based his belief on the fact that when he turned over the body, the feet floated freely to the surface.

When Stewart was asked later why he left the body in the water, he said that it was because, "I didn't think I had no right to pull it out." In this decision Stewart had been joined by two of his crew who were both "superstitious" and didn't want anything to do with touching a dead person. Based on what would happen to some of the others who were involved in this case, these men may have been very wise.

To Stewart's untrained eye there was no sign of a struggle. The clothes on the body were not out of place. Despite the fact that by mid-October the leaves of Washington County are mostly off the trees and the few that remain are a burnt orange, the foliage along the bank of the pond showed no sign of the bushes having been disturbed by a scuffle.

Stewart decided that since there was no helping the victim it was time to call for the sheriff's assistance. It took several minutes for Stewart to climb back up the craggy incline. He got in the town's wagon and went into Cambridge to telephone Washington County Sheriff Samuel Skiff. When Skiff heard the news he immediately called Coroner Millington. Stewart, who throughout the events to follow kept accurate measurements and records of the time, noticed it was 11:00 a.m. when he made the phone call. By the time Stewart returned to the scene, the body had been removed both from the water and the site.

The condition of the log on which the hat and shawl rested would create a long-lasting dilemma. It appears that when Stewart picked up the clothes there was frost on the log under the garments. The existence of frost under the material would mean that the clothes were placed on the log after the frost had already set in for the night. It would also mean that the cloth was cold when it was put down or else it would have melted the frost. The frost was seen as evidence that the hat and shawl were not placed on the log until after 4:00 a.m.

Like in all sensational situations, a sizable crowd gathered soon after Stewart left to get the sheriff. Through a process of self-selection the crowd broke itself into two groups and two locations. One portion, the true voyeurs, managed to struggle down the embankment to be by the body in the brook. The second, those who live to spread news (gossip), remained on the highway, telling the tale to all those who were using the highway this Saturday to shop in Greenwich. (Families that lived west of the village had to pass the site on their way to the village.)

Most of those who saw the body that morning hypothesized that it had been carefully placed in the water. They reached their conclusion based on three telling facts: the position of the corpse, the arrangement of the dress and the condition of the hair. This was a time when proper women wore their hair gathered up near their head. Hair was worn either pinned or in a bun, while the victim's hair was loose. There was no current in the water, so the hair would not have been pulled loose by the flow of the water. The woman's skirt was also down to her ankles. The amateur detectives at the scene felt that if she had walked into the water to commit suicide her skirt would have floated up around her legs. They theorized that she had been lowered into the water while someone held her skirt so the water did not lift the hem. By getting wet from the waist down the skirt would have remained down about her ankles. The final point was the way her arms and hands were positioned. Everyone felt that it looked as if someone had laid her out for the undertaker.

Two men in the crowd,

William "Billy" Wilson and Dick Welch were less timid around a corpse than the members of the road crew. Wilson came by the scene after Stewart had left for help. Wilson, who would play an intriguing role in this story, was driving one of his teams along the road when he saw the gathering crowd. When he was told, by one of those on the road, that someone had drowned, Wilson asked a bystander to hold his team. The man Wilson chose was a neighbor to the scene, a man named Brown. Wilson climbed down the embankment and into the action (in telling the story later he would usually use the term "ran" - an impossibility on this steep slope). When Wilson reached the pond, the woman's body was still floating face down - just as Stewart had left it. Although the two men knew each other, Welch arrived at the scene by himself. With the rock in the water, Wilson and Welch had no trouble reaching the body or in turning over the fragile form. When she was again face up, the two men, like Stewart, noticed that her eyes were closed and her hands were clasped together.

Sheets were brought down

to the shore by one of the neighbors to place under her body when she was removed from the water. Tired of being mere observers Wilson and Welch pulled the body out of the water and up onto the shore. To remove the body from the water each of the men took one of the young girl's arms and dragged her corpse from the pond. As they pulled the corpse out, the interlocked fingers disengaged from each other. As her head came out of the pond a very small amount of water poured from her mouth. The actual amount of water was characterized as being less than a teacupful. Everyone noticed that the girl's natural color returned to her face when the body was turned over. They also noticed that she had a bruise on one finger of each hand.

Although she was neither notorious nor widely known in the area, some of the people in the crowd recognized the victim as Maggie Horrigan, the maid who worked for one of the wealthier men in the community, John Herbert Reynolds. John Reynolds went by the name Herbert. Only one woman, who had gone down the bank near the pond, disagreed with the identification. Later, no one could say who the dissenter was.

When he arrived at the scene, Sheriff Skiff noticed that when Wilson and Welch had taken the body out of the water they had left it so the head was pointed downhill. Afraid that additional water, which could be evidence, might run out of the mouth, Skiff had Wilson help him turn the body around so the head was uphill.

During the early course of events that morning several people who knew Maggie came to the scene. Luckily for later developments in the investigation these people were there before the body was removed from the scene. Among those who knew Maggie and were at the site were: Herbert Reynolds, Maggie's employer, and Chris Coleman, her brother-in-law. Coleman was important because he, like others, noticed that while Maggie's body lay on the shore the collar was still on her dress. During this period, dresses and collars were separate articles. Collars were usually held in place by a button that attached them to the dress. Later that day the collar would inexplicably disappear.

Eventually, Skiff, Wilson and two other men took the body up the bank and placed it in a buckboard. Maggie's body was slowly taken from the scene. It would be years before her spirit would leave the stone bridge. Some say it remained even after they replaced the bridge in the 1960s.

At the time of Maggie's death, the United States was transitioning from an agrarian to an industrial society. To those who lived and worked on farms, Saturday was shopping day. As a result, most people west of Greenwich came into town at some point that day to shop. This traffic caused the news of Maggie's death to disseminate much quicker than it would have on a weekday. When many families finished their shopping on this particular Saturday - even those not living in the direction of the pond - they drove to the site.

Coroner John Millington

was a physician in East Greenwich. He received his call from Sheriff Skiff at about 11 a.m. For reasons never fully explained, it was two hours before he completed the short trip to Greenwich. Millington appointed a coroner's jury to examine the cause of Maggie's death. The authority of the coroner's juries was, at the time, similar to grand juries today. It was common for a coroner's jury to render both a verdict in the cause of death and, if the evidence warranted, suggest who was to blame. In 1889, before the use of photography, in order to deliver a verdict a coroner's jury commonly visited the scene and examined the body. In order to facilitate the process the coroner could legally select the jury without asking for authorization from any other official. In many cases, the coroner's jury was comprised of people who happened to be at the scene or who worked or lived in the area. If a killer stayed around the scene, it is possible that he or she could have been selected to serve on the coroner's jury.

The labyrinth of perplexities of this case are first realized in Coroner Millington's selection of a jury. For reasons not at first obvious he elected not to implement the immediate selection of a jury in this investigation. The coroner's jury in the Maggie Horrigan inquiry was deliberately conscripted and the members had notable political connections.

The coroner's jury

was not selected until approximately 2:00 p.m. The discovery of a body had been reported to Dr. Millington three hours earlier. The members of the jury consisted of: James O. Lavake, who was also the foreman, Amos Griffin, A. A. Young, A. A. Norton, Archie Daisy, H. C. Morhous, John Brooks, and Dr. S. W. Scott. When the jury actually began calling witnesses Scott was no longer a member.

Lavake, Brooks, Griffin, Daisy, and Young were neighbors, living within two blocks of each other. Although Greenwich is small and many could claim to reside within two blocks of each other, these particular two blocks are very significant. The homes are all in the nicest neighborhoods in Greenwich. One has to ask why such an influential group was gathered to examine the cause of death of a mere maid.

Jury members James LaVake and John Brooks resided immediately next to each other at numbers 4 and 6 Church Street. These are two of the more pleasant Victorian homes in the village of Cambridge. Both men listed their occupations in the village directory as commercial travelers (salesmen). In addition to being in sales, LaVake had been elected the county treasurer two years before. Being selected as the county treasurer was even more significant for LaVake, as he was not a native of Washington County. LaVake was born in Castleton, Vermont, but moved with his family to Ohio. During the Civil War, LaVake had served in the 19th Ohio Volunteers. He took part in the battles of Murfreesboro, Chickamaunga, Chattanooga, and Missionary Ridge. LaVake was with Sherman on his march to the sea. At the time of Maggie's death, LaVake was a traveling shoe salesman. In addition to his other responsibilities, LaVake was also the treasurer of the new Consolidated Electric Company. LaVake's neighbor John Brooks was the manager of the same electric company.

Amos Griffin was the third member of the jury who lived on Church Street (number 26). Griffin made his substantial living as an auctioneer.

In what had to be an understatement, Arnold Young listed his occupation as carpenter. He lived at 34 Salem Street in one of the nicer homes in the village. In all probability Young was more of a contractor than just a carpenter. During the Civil War, Young was in the 123rd New York State Volunteers (NYSV) where he served as a musician.

Another member of the jury was a local painter named Albert A. Norton. In the days prior to vinyl siding many men earned their living as house and interior painters. Norton was not just a painter. He also held the political appointment of overseer of the poor. Far more significant, he was an adjutant in the Grand Army of the Republic (GAR). Norton had enlisted in the 123rd NYSV where he had served as a sergeant in the ambulance corp. As adjutant Norton was in a position to influence change. In the period following the Civil War, veterans groups were among the most politically active of any in the community.

The teller of the First National Bank of Greenwich, Archie Daisy, was also selected to serve on the jury. A bank's teller in 1889 was not the same as a teller today. At that time it was one of, if not the most, important positions in the bank, ranking at least at the level of manager and perhaps more often the equivalent of bank president. Tellers lived well and, in small communities such as Greenwich, were among the leading citizens of the village. Daisy was also a collector for the board of education.

The best examples of how significant and political the selection process was, however, were saved for last two members, Henry C. Morhous and Dr. S. W. Scott. Henry Morhous lived slightly more humbly than the other members of the jury residing at 11 Hill Street. Morhous's humility ended at his residence. He was the editor and publisher of *The Peoples Journal* (often referred to as *The Journal*), the community's only newspaper. From almost immediately after the first inquiry that took place, which was held over the two weeks following Maggie's death through a review of the case in 1949, *The Journal* was one of two newspapers that would maintain that her death was a suicide. The position that the death was a suicide was held despite ample testimony, which would cause anyone to question this conclusion.

S. Walter Scott was a licensed physician. Dr. Scott no longer practiced medicine, making his living instead as the owner and manager of the Greenwich Hotel. The Greenwich was on the corner of Bridge and Main Street in the southeastern end of Greenwich. It appears from comments made and reported in the newspapers several months later that Dr. Scott was trying to be as actively involved in the investigation as possible. Dr. Scott was, after all, William Wilson's employer. Wilson was one of the two men who pulled the body from the pond. Dr. Scott had to be removed from the coroner's jury because he volunteered to help with the autopsy.

The Grand Army of the Republic

was formed after the Civil War and was comprised of men who had served in the Union Army. To compare the GAR to the American Legion would not provide the GAR with the true status it held. During the Civil War, the various companies in the Union Army were raised locally. The men in the local unit of the GAR had gone trough the same battles, weather and officers together. Their loyalty to each other was at a level beyond that of the VFW or the American Legion. At the time of this mystery, the GAR was one of the most influential organizations in the region. In Washington County, members of the GAR were almost universally republicans, as were all those holding elected office.

After the jury

viewed the body the remains were removed to Aaron Bristol's Funeral Home for a post-mortem. The jury then called two witnesses, Reuben Stewart and William Wilson to the stand.

As was fairly customary at the time, the funeral business was a second business for Aaron Bristol. Bristol was also a partner in the furniture store of Jones and Bristol located at 23 Main Street.

The Monday newspapers reported that the autopsy indicated that Maggie was not unchaste; therefore, the social need for suicide was eliminated – this was after all the apex of Victorian values and a woman who was pregnant out of wedlock was almost expected to take her own life.

There were several people in the postmortem rooms of undertaker Bristol when the autopsy took place. Dr. Scott, who was originally appointed to the coroner's jury, led the procedure with Dr. George Murray assisting. Coroner Millington was also present but served only as an observer. Bristol, who would be responsible for preparing Maggie's remains for the funeral the next day, was present along with Deputy Sheriff H. B. Teft. The deputy was present during the autopsy because the death was considered to be a possible criminal matter. Teft was responsible for the security of the body until the autopsy was completed.

There was one other person in the room who had no logical or legal reason to be present. Wilson, the man who pulled the body from the water, was in the room at the time of the autopsy. Asked later why he was present, he said he was an undertaker's assistant. He also maintained a livery and worked part-time for Dr. Scott at the hotel.

The coroner's jury agreed to postpone
the remainder of the inquest until after the results of tests pertaining to the contents of Maggie's stomach were received. The jury was interested in the extent the food had been digested. It was already known that Maggie had eaten about 6:00 p.m.; therefore, the extent of digestion would help establish the time of death. This postponement would put off any official findings for a full week.

Late in the afternoon
of October 19th, Doctors S. W. Scott and George Murray conducted an autopsy on the body of Maggie Horrigan. In completing the autopsy they first did an external examination of the body. The doctors' overall impressions were that Maggie was in good health. She appeared to be well nourished and her muscles were well developed. The doctors noted that her skin was more flush than would be anticipated in a corpse. In death, Maggie's hands extended twelve inches in front of her body. The final portion of the external examination was that the pupils of Maggie's eyes were dilated.

The two doctors noted that Maggie's body had four visual marks. There was a cut on the middle finger of her left hand. This distinctive cut appeared to be the result of a fingernail. There was a second abrasion, this one on the knuckle of the ring finger on her right hand. The doctors described this bruise as the "skin was off." There was also a bruise that did not break the skin, on her left cheek. The final abrasions were on her lips. The outside of Maggie's lips had bled a little. Dr. Scott said that he had seen chapped lips that had bled the same amount. There is a conflict in Dr. Scott's report about Maggie's mouth. At one point he said that he did not check the inside of her mouth. This was when he was asked about the bleeding. When he testified a second time he said that there was no cotton in her mouth, which he could have only known if he had examined the inside.

Dr. Scott said at the inquiry that an examination of her mouth failed to show any evidence of cotton. The implication was that she had not been gagged. He also noted that there was froth around her lips. Dr. Murray, who would testify after Dr. Scott at each hearing, did not mention either the cotton or the froth around the mouth. This does not mean that the froth or cotton were there or that they were not, but later developments raise the question of why Dr. Scott made such observations. The froth around Maggie's mouth was believed to be an indication that Maggie had died from asphyxiation.

The doctors then examined Maggie's blood, which they determined was a deeper red than normal - another sign the person had died from lack of air as the blood was seeking oxygen. An external examination of Maggie's lungs indicated that they were inflated. To these two doctors the fact that the lungs were full was considered a symptom of drowning. The doctors knew that the lungs of people who died of other causes were only partially inflated. The doctors made a single incision into one of Maggie's lungs. Although no water was found in Maggie's lung, the doctors agreed that she died as a result of drowning.

In an effort to determine the time of death, the doctors then removed the contents of Maggie's stomach. They first determined that she ate a good meal but not necessarily a hearty meal. What they found was that Maggie's body stopped digesting her dinner less than two hours after she last ate. Dr. Murray used this evidence to establish that the time of death would have been about 7:30 in the evening.

The autopsy ended at 6:15 that evening. The doctors adjourned to Dr. Murray's home where they wrote up their notes. The official results would not be made public for a week; however, the doctors did release the information that Maggie was not "unchaste," therefore she had not committed suicide to hide her shame. With this information out the way plans could be set for her to have a Catholic funeral the next day.

The decision of the coroner's jury, earlier in the day, to postpone the inquiry until after the examination of the contents of the stomach allowed the community to get ahead of the jury. Curiosity being what it is, the public, through rumors and speculation, got way ahead of the jury in the intervening week.

By Saturday evening
there were several stories "of one kind or another" circulating throughout Greenwich. One that was holding a lot of interest related to Dr. Cipperly's son, Abraham. According to the rumors Abraham had heard a woman's scream the night before at about 7:00. The Cipperlys lived just a few houses away from where Maggie resided on the road that led to the bridge. It was understood that Abraham was leading a young colt at the time and could not respond to the scream until he secured the rambunctious young stallion. It was believed young Abraham heard a woman call out something to the effect "No, don't," then her voice went silent or was muffled. Most of the rest of

the tales were considered to be just rumors and speculation.

The fact that forensic science then was much different than today is apparent in an article that appeared in the local paper. *The Journal* gave its first official report the Thursday after the body was found. This article would be much different than the ones they would later publish with its indication that Maggie's death was not a drowning. *The Journal* reminded their patrons that, "the body of any living creature, after drowning, sinks to the bottom and remains there for some days." They went further in suggesting that she did not drown by saying, "her eyes were shut and her body gave no evidence of a struggle, her limbs being straight and her skirts covering her to the feet." It was believed that if a person died as a result of drowning his or her corpse would be drawn up, the legs bent and pulled toward the chest. Although not calling the death a murder, at this point the newspaper felt it was not suicide. This was a position that would later change. The newspaper's assertion at this point is all the more relevant since, as mentioned previously, the editor was one of the people on the coroner's jury.

Henry F. Cipperly

had stayed the night of October 18-19, in Middle Falls with his only brother, Dr. John Cipperly. Henry left for his home early in the morning on the day Maggie's body was discovered. Henry departed so early he had no way of knowing of the young woman's death until he read about it days later in one of the local newspapers. His host, Dr. John Cipperly, was the father of the boy who had heard a woman scream the night before.

When Henry arrived in Easton he came upon a boy, whom he estimated was about fourteen, walking toward Troy. Cipperly knew he was in for a boring journey so he offered the young man a ride.

The boy accepted the generous offer and the two engaged in a rambling conversation until the boy got out at Melrose. Along the way the boy said his family was from Greenwich but told Cipperly that he had been on his own for several months. The boy related two stories that would later become important. First, he told Cipperly that his father maintained a livery business with seventeen blood horses (Wilson was not the boy's father but seems to be the man the boy was imagining as his parent). Second, and even more important, the boy told his benefactor that he had spent the previous night in a barn.

On Sunday, October 20th,

Maggie Horrigan's body was laid out in the front window of Aaron Bristol's Funeral Parlor on Main Street in Greenwich. Bristol, knowing the community's interest, had the body on display by the time the sun rose. During the course of the morning, a large crowd gathered at both the window and inside the parlor to pay their final respect to the pretty young girl. In keeping with her humble existence, more people would know Maggie in death than in life.

One of those who saw Maggie's remains that day was a young schoolgirl about twelve years old. This girl had known Maggie when she was alive and was captivated by her persona. We know of their relationship from a letter that the child wrote when she was an elderly woman. In the letter, the woman remembered Maggie as being a tall, beautiful person. We also know from reading this letter that Maggie must have had patience with children. The week before Maggie died she had visited an uncle who lived on the south side of Middle Falls. While at her uncle's, Maggie had made this girl feel special by taking the young adolescent for a walk. A twelve-year-old girl out with a nineteen-year-old young woman - no wonder the younger girl would remember the night for the rest of her life. For their outing Maggie had gone with the young girl to watch the evening train come into the station. Our expectations in entertainment have come a long way in a hundred years.

On that Sunday morning, as the young girl looked in Bristol's window, she was struck by the sight of Maggie's fingers. Bristol's had arranged Maggie's hands across her chest in a traditional pose. The young girl fixated on one of the fingers on each hand. These hands would be forever established in her mind. Just as was found in the autopsy the girl noticed that one

of the fingers showed a cut like it had been injured by someone's fingernail. A finger on the other had showed a skinned
knuckle.

By prior arrangement, at 10:00 a.m. Maggie's body was
moved to St. Joseph's Roman Catholic Church on Hill Street in
Greenwich for her funeral service. The church was founded in
1868. In the 1880s the church was enlarged and a pastoral residence added. At the time of Maggie's funeral, the church
boasted over one thousand members.

Father Field, who had been the parish's priest since
1879, and Maggie's confessor, presided over the service. Like
Maggie, Father Field was Irish, having been born in County
Cork. Father Field is said to have provided a just tribute to the
young maid. He also used unequivocal terms when he told
those gathered that Maggie's death was not suicide. Father
Field advised those in attendance that Maggie was a good
Catholic and thus would never have taken her own life. Field
had every reason to believe in Maggie, as she had walked the
two miles from her home to the church to attend services every
Sunday. Maggie and her young female friends went together
and often members of Maggie's family met them at the church.
By the time of the funeral it was also known from the autopsy
that Maggie had died a virgin.

It is generally accepted, but undocumented, that during
his words for Maggie Father Fields called for a curse on those
who had taken the life of such a beautiful, virtuous Catholic
lass.

After the service in Greenwich, undertaker Aaron
Bristol took Maggie's body to her home community of
Cambridge where she was buried that day in St. Patrick's
Cemetery. The wagon ride probably took a little over an hour,

as the communities are only seven and a half miles apart. Maggie was buried in the same plot as her mother and younger brother. It was intended that from that moment forward the three would spend an uninterrupted eternity together. This was not the case.

Visiting the site

where all the action had taken place the day before was the thing to do after church on the Sunday morning of Maggie's funeral. With morbid curiosity, many families left whatever services they had attended in Cambridge, Middle Falls and Argyle and went to the site where Maggie's body had been discovered. It was as if the location had suddenly been transformed into an amusement park. People climbed down the steep bank and walked to the site where the wet body had rested just a day before. The visit of this throng destroyed any evidence that may have remained after the curiosity seekers had departed the day before. One thing they all would have noticed was a path leading up a different portion of the bank to a barn at the top of the hill.

By Sunday morning rumors as to what had happened to Maggie the previous Friday night were running rampant. Everyone was speculating as to the cause of death. The simple circumstances relating to the cause of death were not enough to nurture the hunger of the rabble that feeds on gossip. For those who felt the cause was murder, and that was the majority, they expanded their suppositions to include reckless speculation as to the identity of the perpetrator(s). In addition to the identity of the perpetrator(s), the gossip circle could not withstand an opportunity to add conjecture as to the motive. In short, the community was alive with accusation, scandal and chatter. In just twenty-four hours Greenwich had been transformed from a safe haven to a place of notoriety, fear and anxiety.

Men who had stayed at home the Friday night before were suddenly grateful that they led uneventful lives, as were the men who had an indisputable alibi for their whereabouts. Those men who had been out and about were actively trying to remind those who had seen them that fateful evening of exactly when and where they had been seen. It was a time when the men of the region were consumed in the effort of establishing where they were at the time Maggie died.

Friday, October 18th,

was a typical workday for nineteen-year-old Maggie Horrigan. No one, not even her assailants, could guess the extent of the tragedy that would follow that evening. To most it appeared that one life was wasted. In fact it was many lives that were destroyed that one day. Maggie died but others would be persecuted by the memory of the deed they had performed.

Maggie was employed in the beautiful red brick house on the road through Middle Falls. She was the domestic servant for the widow Mrs. Mary Reynolds and her unmarried son Herbert. The situation was slightly unusual because of the two additional people in the house. Mrs. Reynolds widowed daughter, forty-eight year-old Mary McMaster and her grown daughter, twenty-two year-old Mary Lena McMaster were "staying over" at the house. Since all three Reynolds women were named Mary, the mother went by Mrs. Reynolds, the daughter by Mary, and the granddaughter, Mary Lena, went by Lena.

Mrs. McMaster and her daughter, Lena, lived in a house only two miles from her brother's residence. The McMaster's residence was on what is now Main Street in Greenwich. Even though it would be a short trip home, often the pair would stay over when Mary visited her mother and brother. They came about every three to four weeks and would stay for two to four days. Their visits, although not a regular event, were common enough that they did not truly count as guests.

Although it was not celebrated, the previous day had marked the thirteen-month anniversary of the day Maggie came to work for Mrs. Reynolds and her son. Maggie had told several people that she was content in her employment and planned to spend the winter working at the Reynolds's house. Prior to her employment with the Reynolds family, Maggie had worked for three years as a servant for a family named McGeough in Shushan.

As the only domestic in the house, Maggie was required to complete virtually all of the household chores. Her duties went from building the fire in the morning to baking bread and doing the laundry. In effect the Reynoldses had hired the equivalent of a farmer's wife. One chore that received attention was fetching water from the well in the front yard. This was a cumbersome task so Maggie often did it early in the morning. It required appreciable strength to carry the buckets of water from the front of the house to the kitchen. As a result of her duties, Maggie had become a very muscular young woman.

As sunset was setting in, Maggie made the family's dinner, which included a treat of out of season berries for dessert. To keep the cost of lighting by gas lamps down most people ate soon after dusk. Maggie ate by herself in the kitchen while the family ate in the dining room. After the family finished supper she served tea, then set about doing her after dinner cleaning chores.

This Friday Maggie had made plans to take a walk around the hamlet with three of her friends. The girls were to meet at around 7:00 p.m., so she hurried to finish her task. She washed the dinner dishes except the drinking glasses. When it was learned that Maggie had left the glasses unwashed, some, who believed her death was a suicide, thought the dirty glasses were a sign that she was distracted. In a time before running water and on demand hot water, Maggie often left the drinking glasses to be washed in fresh water the next morning. Maggie was generally done with her chores in the house by 6:30. After that she would then take less than half an hour to run her outside errands.

After dinner, and before her evening stroll, Maggie usually walked to a local grocery for fresh milk. Although the family heard her going about her chores and leaving for milk, none of them would ever see Maggie alive after she served the evening's tea.

Later in the evening she would usually meet some combination of three friends her own age for an evening stroll. This group of young ladies included Miss Julia Nolan and the Obenauer sisters. Maggie and her female friends would go to the post office to check for mail. In all small communities checking for mail each evening was really only a front for visiting. The post office of any small town in the evening was a chance to see and be seen. It was a daily opportunity to catch up on the gossip. When a person least wanted it, getting the mail was also the opportunity to be the brunt of the chatter.

There would be some debate about what happened to Maggie that evening. All that is being presented in this section is that which is universally accepted as true. The events in question are left for later.

On Friday night, October 18th,

Maggie did not show up as anticipated for the evening walk with her group of young women. After only a few minutes Julia Nolan went to the Reynolds kitchen door to inquire as to Maggie's whereabouts. To get to the kitchen door Julia had to go through the woodshed attached to the back of the house. The kitchen door was the one Maggie usually used when she left or entered the house and Julia was used to using it also. By using this door the family was not disturbed by the servant's coming and going.

Mrs. McMaster happened to be in the kitchen and answered the door when Julia knocked. Before answering

Julia's inquiry as to Maggie's whereabouts, Mrs. McMaster turned and noticed two containers of fresh milk, then called to her brother. Hearing Herbert's response that he thought Maggie had gone out, Mary McMaster told Julia that Maggie was not home. Not finding Maggie, Julia left the house through the woodshed.

So consistent were Maggie's habits that no one in the Reynolds household bothered to look at the clock as they heard Maggie go about her chores. It was the time of wooden floors and area carpets. Keep in mind that this was before radios, television or other external noises. People could keep track of family members by the sounds they made in the house.

At about 6:45 Maggie had gone down to the Widow Patton's store to pick up milk for the next day. Knowing Maggie would come during the evening, if Mrs. Patton felt like closing early, she would leave the Reynolds family milk in a side door. On these occasions Maggie would leave the empty pail and pick up the following day's supply. She didn't need money, as Mrs. Patton would just add the cost to the Reynolds account. At some later time the money would be paid. After all, if anyone was good for a debt it was the Reynolds family. Several different people saw Maggie as she walked to the store but only one, Rosa Alwell, spoke to her.

Margaret "Maggie" Horrigan's family

lived in the nearby community of Cambridge. Maggie was born there in 1870. She was the second child of John Horrigan and Katherine "Kate" Flarrity. Her parents had migrated to the United States prior to the birth of her older sister, Mary. John and Kate were both born in Ireland. John in 1840, and Kate in 1843. John was a farmer earning his living on a rented farm in the town of Cambridge, Washington County.

The Horrigan's had five children. Their ages at the time of Maggie's death were Mary, twenty; Maggie, nineteen; James, seventeen; and Thomas, age eleven. The other brother, John, had died in 1882; he would have been fourteen when Maggie died. The mother, Kate, died in 1878 at the age of thirty-five. This was the same year Thomas was born and her death was probably due to complications relating to his birth. By the time Maggie died, John and their mother were both interred in St. Patrick's Cemetery just outside the village of Cambridge. They did not have individual head stones but shared one obelisk. Maggie's body would join their space.

On September 27, 1886, at the age of seventeen, Mary Horrigan, Maggie's sister, married twenty-five year-old Christopher Coleman. Coleman was a baker by trade. Christopher was originally from Lansingburgh, his parents both being of Irish extraction. The young couple had no children of their own but, at the time of Maggie's death, were raising Mary's youngest brother, Thomas. John Horrigan only had one child, his son James, still living home.

Maggie Horrigan

was one of the many unmarried young Irish maids hired by old-line American families whose values would not allow them to be perceived as almost wealthy. These families wanted to have the luxuries and privileges that their hard work and investments had earned but were concerned about "appearances." The year was 1889; Europe and the major cities of America were going through a period of social adjustment. It was the beginning of the Gilded Age, with its opulent lifestyle. In other places the new super rich were living in splendor, building palaces in Saratoga and Newport and creating a new economic aristocracy. The values of the Gilded Age were in direct conflict with the strict moral code of the late Victorian Era.

The conflict in values was less obvious to those who lived in rural areas such as Washington County. In these rural New England communities the citizens were ingrained in a culture formed and still wrapped in the Calvinist values of hard work and humility – it was essential to at least present those values to those on the outside. The cultural mores in rural America were part of the religious values that, when the colonies were being settled, had brought many immigrants from England to America. As a result of the social climate of Middle Falls, Maggie had worked hard, but not unreasonably hard, for over a year in a household that lived well but not extravagantly.

In the customs of the day, Maggie was considered comely. She was five foot six inches tall with long red hair. She had several dresses. Some she considered her work dresses, while others were worn on special occasions such as going to church. Her weight was put at between one hundred and forty and one hundred and fifty pounds, which would have made her slightly rubenesque, a real treat for this period. Her chores required that she use her strength frequently, so much so that she was considered muscular. Her physical appearance was at the very least above average and in all likelihood she would be described as beautiful.

Maggie was a devout Catholic and attended Mass every Sunday. Weekly attendance was even more of a challenge as she had to walk over two miles each way to attend services. Yet she went every week despite the issue of weather.

When Maggie was fourteen,
she hired out to be a housekeeper. She was employed as a domestic continuously for the next five years. The position of household servant was favorable for Maggie as she was allowed

to live in the homes where she worked. As a condition of employment, she was provided room and board. Being a household servant provided her with a good clean residence and in the case of her current employment a reasonable working environment.

Porter Reynolds,

when he was alive, had listed his occupation as a farmer but was really a true agricultural manager. Maggie worked for his widow and their son Herbert. Porter had, in fact, made part of his money as the keeper of a hotel. The Reynolds family was a classic example of the real old-line American family. They were of English extraction and had originally settled in Rhode Island. Near the end of the eighteenth century, Porter's father and grandfather had come to North Greenwich to built and operate a hotel. This hotel became a stagecoach tavern, a respite for those on the long tedious ride north. Near the time of his death Porter was reported to have been one of the wealthiest farmers in the county, having over one thousand acres of farmland. During Porter's lifetime, the family employed five hands and three domestic servants.

Porter had married into a family with roots at least as deep as his own. He married Mary Sherman Remington. Mary's family was quick to remind people that her grandfather, David Remington, was a soldier in the Revolutionary War. Porter and Mary Reynolds had six children. Two had moved out of the area and three remained in Washington County. Andrew had moved to Indiana. Merritt lived in California. Amander Porter died fairly young. Three other children still lived in the immediate area. Mary had married William McMaster of Lockport. He died prior to 1880 and Mary had returned to her hometown of Greenwich to finish raising her two children,

Porter and Mary Lena. John Herbert never married and never left his parents' home. At the time Maggie disappeared, Herbert was living with his mother in the house where Maggie worked. For a period about the time of the Civil War, Herbert had owned a general store in Middle Falls but had sold out to his brother Pitt and now considered himself a still life and landscape artist.

Pitt owned one of the hotels in Middle Falls and lived in a house on the road to Bald Mountain. Pitt's red brick house was on situated almost directly behind his brother and mother's house, on the road behind the family homestead.

Maggie was described

by the Reynoldses as cheery and pleasant. They considered her in high terms for a domestic, remarking on how she talked very little in the house. To them she was an unassuming girl with a good disposition and pleasant personality. On a point that would later make a difference in how people envisioned her death, the family said Maggie never complained about her health. They said that the only time she had been sick while in their employ was the previous spring. At that time, she had been treated by Dr. Gray. The Reynoldses never heard Maggie utter words that would imply in any way that she was depressed or tired of life.

Maggie had three close friends and several other associates. Her closest friend, Julia Nolan, saw Maggie slightly differently than the Reynoldses. She said that she had always seen Maggie in a happy disposition until the Tuesday before her death. That evening the two girls had gone for their customary stroll to the post office. On this occasion, Maggie told Julia that she had not felt well all summer. When Julia asked the nature of the problem Maggie said that she had seen Dr. Gray and he had said she did not digest her food properly. Maggie had continued her tale telling Julia that Dr. Gray's diagnosis was supported by an "Indian doctor" who she saw when he came to Greenwich with the fair. Julia had asked if Maggie had taken all of the *Sagwa* (Native American medicinal compounds). Maggie had said she had not finished the medicine, then went on to say that she "almost wished she was dead." Julia had admonished Maggie for her comment but Maggie insisted that was how she felt. Julia would be resolute throughout the investigations that this was the one and only time Maggie ever talked of wishing her life was over.

Maggie's father described her as amiable and having a happy disposition. Her father said she was strongly attached to her church and faithful to her religious observance. He assured reporters at one of the inquiries that she would never have committed suicide.

There is no doubt that Maggie was a beautiful, physically strong and virtuous young woman, traits that may have actually contributed to her death.

On Friday evening, October 18th,
many who lived in Middle Falls were out. These people noted that it was unusual for Maggie not to be walking with Julia. Usually the girls would meet and first walk to the post office, then either call upon a neighbor or return to one of their residences and visit for a while. Maggie was very conscious of her reputation and was home each evening by 9:00.

In the entire time Maggie had worked for the Reynoldses, she had spent only one night out of the house. That night was the previous summer when she slept at the home of Julia Nolan. Even that night Maggie had sent word to the Reynoldses that she would not be home.

In thinking about

it later, Mrs. McMaster could remember nothing distinctive about the evening until about 7:00 p.m. when Julia Nolan arrived at the door asking about Maggie. The noises Maggie normally made in the kitchen were heard that evening. When Maggie went for milk each evening, she used the woodshed door, so she would not have passed the family on either her way out or when she returned to the house. Somewhere between 7:20 and 8:00 p.m. the Obenauer girls came to the dining room door again asking about Maggie. Mary was reasonably certain of the time as she had just gone to her room upstairs.

Lena went to bed about 9:30 and Herbert at 10:00. Mary's mother, the elderly Mrs. Reynolds, was worried about Maggie. Mrs. Reynolds stayed up until 11:00 p.m. waiting for Maggie. Finally, Mrs. Reynolds decided that Maggie must be spending the night with a girlfriend and went to bed.

It was the next morning

when Mary McMaster first became mindful that Maggie had not come home the previous evening. At 7:00 a.m. Mary had come downstairs and found her brother starting the wood fire in the kitchen stove – building the fire would have been one of Maggie's chores each cold morning. Since there was only one occasion in her thirteen months of working for the Reynoldses that Maggie had not spent the night in the house, the family was troubled about her whereabouts. Throughout the morning, members of the Reynolds family commented to each other on her absence. Their comments went on until about 11:00 a.m. when the Reynoldses heard of the discovery of her body in the pond. In one of the inquiries, Mary pointed out that her brother, Herbert, made no more fuss than any other member of the family. Even more important he had not made any explanation for Maggie's absence. The question in everyone's mind was the degree Herbert, a single man, was involved in what ever happened to Maggie.

In testimony that they would all be required to give, Mary McMaster, her daughter, Lena, and her brother Herbert all told the justice that they had seen nothing unusual in Maggie's behavior that day and none of the them felt she was depressed.

That same night, in Fort Edward,
a carriage had been rented to four men each of whom enjoyed some local prominence. The group was known to enjoy an evening out. When the team was returned much later that night the horses were "well lathered." Word of the heated horses spread through the village's gossip network. The story of the horses was carried in low voices for fear the wrong persons might misinterpret the reason for their condition. After all, the men were reported to have witnesses that they would say they were in Glens Falls that evening. If it had not been for the coincidence that it was the same night that Maggie was murdered, the incident may have gone unnoticed.

Map of Middle Falls

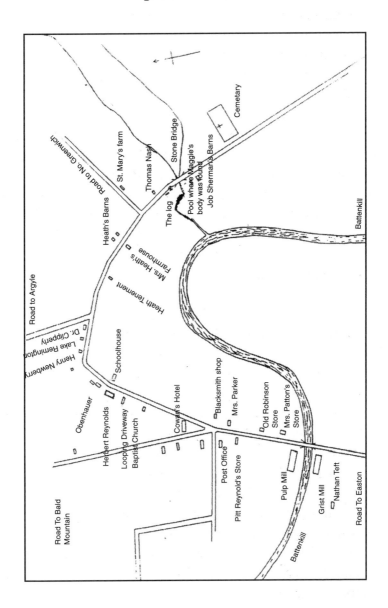

Middle Falls

was originally called Galesville. Attracted to the abundant waterpower, Abram Lansing, for whom a school is named in Cohoes, initially settled at the site of the hamlet along the banks of the Battenkill before 1800, some reports put the date in the 1790s. Lansing built a house and mill along the falls, on the Greenwich side of the river. At this time a mill wheel would have many uses based primarily on the season. In the fall, the power would have been transferred through a series of belts to stones used for grinding flour. In the spring, a second set of belts would have transferred the power to a sawmill. Lansing eventually sold the mill to Joseph Heath who enlarged the facility.

Once settlement started in the area, in the late 1790s until the middle of the 1850s, people would take their picnic baskets and ride up to the "kill" for a pleasant outing among the dells along the banks of the river with the falls as a backdrop. Over a period of fifty years this picturesque setting slowly changed so that the beauty of the natural falls became but a line in the sequence of water powered factories and mills.

John Gale, after whom the hamlet was initially named, built the Galesville Woolen Mill on the south side of the kill in 1847. This mill produced a wide variety of woolen products that were primarily sold locally. During the Civil War, John Gale built a flourmill on the opposite side of the kill. A competing mill was built about the same time.

Over time, several more plants were built all because of the abundant resource of the power of the waterfalls.
• The Ondawa Paper Company was formed in 1882. This company employed thirty-five operatives and boasted a monthly payroll of $1,800.

- Also on the banks of the falls was the Bennington Falls Pulp & Paper Company, incorporated in 1884. The man who later officiated over a portion of the inquiry into Maggie's death, Henry Mansfield, was the treasurer of the company. His daughter-in-law's father, whose house would be used for part of the hearing, W. N. Sprague, was the president of the plant. The company's primary product was manila paper.
- M. Crandall of Middle Falls was the superintendent of the Battenkill Paper Company. This was a second paper company near the Bennington facilities.
- Near the site of the other factories, the Middle Falls Manufacturing Company produced leatherboard, mill and shank.
- The ultimate demise of all of these plants was predicated on the product of the newly created power plant. The Greenwich Electric Light and Power Company was furnishing the newly established electric lights for the villages of Greenwich, Schuylerville, Cambridge, Victory Mills and Middle Falls. J. O. Lavake was the treasurer of the power company. Lavake was one of the members of the coroner's jury.

The Cipperly & Hegeman's flour and plaster mill and a sawmill joined these plants.

With mills came taverns and hotels. Nathan Teft's tavern and Crowner's Hotel just south of the house where Maggie worked were the principle watering holes for those who finished work with a thirst.

In 1837 the community built a Baptist church just south of the Reynolds's house.

By 1889, where there had been no one a hundred years before, there were now five hundred residences in Middle Falls. It was a typical hamlet for its time in that the citizens of Middle

Falls were very interconnected. The working class lived in tenements better than most but still nowhere near as nice as the homes of the managers. Single men and women lived in boarding houses that were set up only for one gender. There existed houses with bad reputations and places where distilleries manufactured bootleg whiskey. There was a strict social code, those "with" married those "with" - and those "without" married those "without." Thus there was maintained a social structure.

The electricity generated by the new power plant would in time take away the need to have factories adjacent to waterpower. With the advent of electricity, the new variable in selecting a location for factories became access to the railroads. With time entropy set in on all the mills in Middle Falls and one by one they closed.

As fast as it had evolved, Middle Falls's growth was hindered by its proximity to Greenwich. Greenwich had grown faster and offered more services. Although Greenwich would be considered industrial in its own right, it was more the residential and commercial center and Middle Falls the base of industry. Many people walked each day from their homes in Greenwich to their employment in Middle Falls.

Map of Greenwich

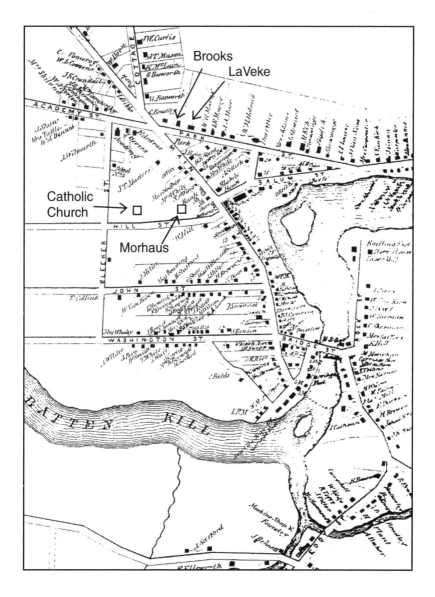

The first inquiry

into the cause of Maggie's death began the day her body was discovered and continued on the next two weekends. The probe that took place that first day was minimal, appearing to be little more than just a surface inspection. The remainder of the first public inquiry fell into two distinct sessions - each was two days long and each had a fairly clear objective. A second public inquiry would be pursued several months later and, like the first, fell into distinct sessions.

The coroner's jury opened its inquiry the afternoon Maggie's body was found. Although there is no evidence that the jury went to the pond, the members did go to Bristol's funeral parlor to examine Maggie's remains.

Probably on the advice of Dr. Millington, the jury members agreed that an autopsy was needed to help them arrive at both the cause and time of death. The jury, knowing that an analysis of the stomach and autopsy would take time and having viewed the body, adjourned the inquiry for one week so that the two forensic examinations could be completed.

On the first day the jury heard briefly from two witnesses each of whom had been at the pond that morning. Reuben Stewart, the man who had made the initial discovery, told of the events that morning that led to the finding of Maggie's body. Stewart was followed by Will Wilson, the man who helped pull Maggie's remains from the pond. Wilson told the jury the position and condition of the body as he helped extract it from the shallow water.

Although the formal inquiry was in abeyance after these two witnesses, the natural curiosity of the community kept the incident stirring in the week between the discovery of Maggie's body and the next meeting of the coroner's jury. The witnesses called in the second session indicated that the people believed that the person responsible was a single man and probably of Irish dissent.

On Saturday the 26th,

one full week after Maggie's death, the coroner's jury reconvened. There didn't appear to be a rush to find out what had occurred, as the examination of witnesses didn't begin until 2:00 p.m. on the eighth day after her body was found. On this day, Washington County District Attorney Edgar Hull came by train from Fort Edward to lead the examination. Detective Price of the Pinkerton Agency accompanied the district attorney to Greenwich.

The inquiry this day centered on the cause of death. It was, therefore, only natural that the testimony began with Dr. S. Walter Scott who had directed the autopsy, followed by Dr. George Murray who had assisted. The only two others to testify that day were the men who found and removed the body from the water, Reuben Stewart and Will Wilson. This was the second time these two had testified in public.

The testimony of the two doctors started with what had been learned as a result of the autopsy they had completed the previous Saturday. Their initial testimony followed the information that was reported in the section discussing the autopsy. There were follow-up questions asked of each of the doctors by District Attorney Hull, Coroner Millington and members of the jury. These questions indicated the perceptions of the jury. It appears from the questions that some jurors wanted to be sure the cause was drowning, not asphyxiation by some other method.

On the stand, Dr. Scott added to his statement from the written autopsy that the froth found on Maggie's mouth and nose was finer than that found on bodies where the person died of causes other than drowning. He emphasized strongly his belief that the froth was direct proof that she had died from drowning. So certain was Dr. Scott that drowning was the cause of Maggie's death that he told the jurors that other potential reasons were not investigated. The issue of drowning was important to Dr. Scott, as it was a clear indication that the probable cause of death was suicide.

One juror questioned the doctor as to the differences that would be observed on a body that died from smothering than one that died of drowning. Dr. Scott answered that there would be no differences except the presence of water in the lungs. Having a second idea, he then elaborated, stating that Maggie's stomach had more water than normal, perhaps as much as twice the normal amount. Dr. Scott felt the only possible cause of the additional water would have been the intake during drowning. Then Scott added that he and Dr. Murray were satisfied in their own minds that there was froth in the passageways so they only made one surgical opening into the lungs. Dr. Scott admitted that there was no water found as a result of that incision.

There is no explanation as to why there was not a follow-up to the conflict in Dr. Scott's testimony. At one point, he says that the froth would have been present in any death by asphyxiation. Later, he said that the only difference between a drowning and a smothering would be the presence of water in the lungs. Still later, he held that no water was found in the lungs. Somehow Dr. Scott reasoned that the cause of death had to be drowning. It was as if he had accepted the fact first and made the evidence fit the theory rather than let the evidence develop the theory.

In front of the coroner's jury, Dr. Murray contradicted his counterpart on two major points. First, he acknowledged that he only noted a little more liquid in the stomach than would have been considered normal, not twice the normal amount that Dr. Scott said he had found. Second, and for reasons not explored further, Dr. Murray told the coroner's jury that the lack of water in the lungs was a good indication that she was not put in the water after death. It is amazing but, there was no explanation as to why, in Dr. Murray's mind, the lack of water indicated drowning.

Dr. Murray told the coroner's jury that, in his opinion, based on the extent of digestion of the contents of the stomach, Maggie had died about 7:30 p.m. the evening before her body was found. On a follow-up question the doctor revised his time to a range noting that it could have been as late as 10:00 p.m.

One significant point in Dr. Murray's examination that day came when he affirmed that he had never performed an autopsy on a person who had died as a result of drowning. The conclusion he reached on Maggie's death would therefore have been either on the advice of Dr. Scott or as a result of reviewing his college texts.

That same day Reuben Stewart was called as a witness. He again told the jury of the discovery of Maggie's body and his actions and those of others at the scene. Stewart escaped excessive questioning by Hull or the jurors. It looks as though Stewart was considered to be just the poor unfortunate soul who happened upon the body.

Like Stewart, Wilson was asked for his account of what happened on that fateful day the previous week. Wilson told the jury how he was driving one of his teams down the road when he heard from a pedestrian that someone had drowned. Wilson went on to tell of the position of Maggie's body when he began removing it from the water. Wilson, unlike Stewart, was asked a series of follow-up questions. First, the jurors wanted to know who else was present at the pond that morning. He informed the jury that he did not know everyone that was there or even everyone that lived in the neighborhood of the millpond. Wilson was asked if anyone present the morning the body was found said that the remains were not those of Maggie Horrigan. He told the jury that some woman at the scene did say it was not Maggie but he did not know the identity of the person. At the hearing, no one asked Wilson why he was present during the autopsy or why he happened to come by the site where Maggie was found. After Wilson testified the coroner's jury adjourned until Monday afternoon, the 28th.

If we are to believe a letter Hull wrote five years later, he ordered a second autopsy that afternoon in an effort to receive a more definitive cause of death. It was apparent that those in the inquiry were not as convinced as Dr. Scott that Maggie drowned herself.

When the coroner's jury reconvened on Monday, Edgar Hull was not present. The investigation was led by forty-three year-old James White, a private attorney from Greenwich. Hull's absence is not explained in the record but we do know that the following week was the county elections. Hull was up for reelection and he may have had campaign commitments that day. Then again, there may have been a deeper and far more sinister reason why he avoided the public investigation.

There was a definite difference in presentation and presence between Hull and White. Edgar Hull appeared cold and impersonal. He had cold, beady eyes that were even more conspicuous because his baldhead provided no distraction from their icy glare. He was not part of the community and, therefore, was not under direct pressure to examine any specific witness. White, in contrast, was a part of the political and social structure of the village. He could not help but be privy to the local gossip, rumors and conjecture. White also had a fatherly quality, seeming more judge-like. He would reflect on the facts rather than jump to conclusions. Though on at least one occasion during the investigation, White showed that he had a temper when provoked.

Under the administration of White, the focus of the investigation shifted from the cause of Maggie's death to the reason and potential suspects. It is obvious from the witnesses called that White held a belief that the person responsible for her death knew Maggie. It also appears he felt the perpetrator was most likely a jilted or rejected lover. The first three witnesses called were all age-appropriate single men who lived in the vicinity of the Reynolds's house.

Since the Irish

were pretty much at the bottom of the social ladder in the area, twenty-three year-old William Scully, an Irish immigrant, had the dubious distinction of being the first witness on Monday. It was obvious from some of the questions that Scully was considered an attractive marriage prospect. Some of the questions that would be asked of other witnesses implied that it was rumored that Maggie had a crush on Scully. White spent quite some time trying to connect Scully to Maggie via an intimate social relationship.

In June 1887, a little over two years before the death of Maggie, William Scully had come to this country from Ireland. Upon arrival in America, Scully followed the migration pattern of many of his countrymen. He first lived in New York City.

46

Later he moved to Washington County where he worked for various families as a farm helper. During his brief life in the county, he had also been employed by two of the mills in Middle Falls.

There were a series of questions asked as to Scully's residence and employment. It was inconvenient for Scully that, on the same day Maggie's body was found, he moved into the tenement of Thomas Nash. Thomas Nash and his family lived directly across the road from the millpond. Scully had known the Nash family in Ireland, with   Mrs. Nash being his first cousin. He had also visited at the Nash home several times during the period since he had moved to Washington County. It was his visits to the Nashes that caused the investigation to center on him this morning. One of the issues was the number of times Scully had stayed with the Nashes. He had stayed there many times. Scully may have stayed at the Nashes so often because, prior to September, he had been living on farms. Although no one would consider the location of the Nash home to be in a village, it did offer far greater social opportunities than a rural house. There was an unfortunate irony in the fact that Maggie visited Mrs. Nash several times while Scully was at the house.

Before the coroner's jury, Scully was called upon to account for his activities on the day Maggie died. Scully, who had just become unemployed, had left the home of James Marshal at seven in the morning looking for work. He first went to visit one of his previous employers, Ephraim Lewis. He stayed and "visited" with the Lewises for about two hours, leaving at 10:00 a.m. He then went to visit with another previous employer, James Mulligan, and from there he went to the home of a friend, Mrs. Quilty. Scully told the jury that he stayed at

Mrs. Quilty's until 5:30 then he went to the home of his friend Thomas O'Donnell where he "stayed the night."

Before Maggie's body was found the next morning, Scully left O'Donnell's about seven bound for Nash's tenement. At 9:00 a.m. Scully and O'Donnell each drove a team from Nash's house to Schuylerville to pick up two loads of coal for Nash. It was 4:00 that afternoon that Scully learned of Maggie's death.

The line of questioning then shifted as the coroner's jury tried to develop a personal link between Maggie and Scully. Scully may have been nervous or he may not have understood the linkage the coroner was going for, but he gave different answers during the questioning. At first he said that Maggie had stopped at the Nash home about three times on her way to church. He said he had never seen her anywhere else but at the Nash home. Later he raised the number of times Maggie stopped by to four or five. More important to the tenor of the investigation, he insisted that he never "waited on Maggie." Later he told of having walked her to the Nolan house one afternoon the previous summer. While they were at the Nolans's Maggie had mistakenly introduced Scully as Mr. Nash – in this answer Scully was trying to show he and Maggie were not close. The two had stayed at the Nolans's for about two hours. When they left Scully and Maggie "took the short walk," the path over the small hill between the Bald Mountain road and the Reynolds's home. White tried to extend the amount of time Maggie had spent with Scully that afternoon. To reassure those inquiring as to his activities and intent, Scully told the jury that he was certain that he was at Thomas Nash's for dinner the day of the walk.

One of the principal complexities of this mystery is

Maggie's reported fear of the dark. The witnesses all told of her anxiety if required to be out by herself at night. This caused the question as to why she was outside alone in the dark the night she disappeared. Scully assured the jury that he never saw Maggie out after dark alone.

The final line of questions went to the possibility that Maggie had other gentlemen callers. To Scully's knowledge the beautiful Maggie had no admirers. Scully assured the court he knew nothing of men walking her to church either through having seen them or rumor.

The last time Scully had seen Maggie alive was the Sunday evening before her death. She and Julia Nolan passed the Nash house on their way home from church. Scully had been sitting on the porch and the girls saluted him. He saluted them back.

Timothy Nash,

the younger brother of Thomas Nash, followed Scully on the stand. Timothy worked in the pulp mill in Middle Falls. He passed the Reynolds's house twice each day on his way to and from work. Even though he was single, Timothy was quickly removed as a suspect when he told the court that he had been at work in the mill from five the evening Maggie died until seven the next morning. Timothy admitted that Maggie had stopped at his brother's about "five or six times" on her way to or from church. Like Scully, he had not called on Maggie nor did he know of any other male callers. The only incriminating portion of his testimony was that on the day Maggie's body was found he said Scully arrived at his brother's at 10:00 a.m., an hour later than Scully had reported he left for Schuylerville.

Edmond Boyd

was the next witness. Because he started by trying to diminish his attraction to Maggie, Boyd had the greatest problems with the questioning. Boyd was a native of Georgia who had migrated north looking for employment. For the previous five years he had worked as a mechanic at the Ondawa Paper Mill. Boyd boarded in Middle Falls just north of the bridge at the home of the Widow Patten.

The previous winter Boyd had gone to the home of Mrs. Andrews in Greenwich to "call on" Maggie's cousin Jose Quilty. While he was at the Andrews's house Boyd was introduced to one of the other guests in the house, Maggie Horrigan. With darkness as early as it is in the winter the line of questioning went to whether Maggie was accompanied on the way to and from the Andrews's. Boyd told the jury he was uncertain how Maggie came or left the Andrews's but was certain that other young women were at the house at the same time. Thus implying that Maggie had been escorted by someone on her walk to Greenwich.

The line of questioning then switched to Boyd's activities on the night of October 18th. Before the jury, Boyd acknowledged that he walked the two miles to "the show" in Greenwich. To get there on time Boyd had left his boarding house at approximately 6:45. He stopped at the post office and then Pitt Reynolds's store before going on alone to Greenwich. In Boyd's estimation the two stops only took five minutes.

On his way out of Middle Falls, he walked up the left side of the road to a point referred to as the "ordinary crossing." He then crossed back over the road to the right side. As he came to the stone bridge Boyd saw what he thought was a young woman walking very slowly. In Boyd's opinion she looked as if she was waiting for someone on the bridge. Because the woman was on the same side as he, when he got about fifteen feet from her he switched sides of the road for second time. Like any man seeing a woman out alone on a dark night, Boyd watched the woman as he passed. Boyd told the jurors that he felt she turned her head away from him as he went by. Based on the woman's size and, what in the dark Boyd believed to be a white feather in her hat, he thought at the time the woman was Maggie. Although he knew Maggie well, Boyd made no attempt to talk to the person on the bridge. This may well have been because he felt that if she was out at a place like the bridge alone at night, then she did not want to be recognized.

Just after Boyd crossed the bridge, he heard a horse-drawn carriage coming up behind him. In an effort to determine if the carriage held the woman's escort, he slowed his walk down but did not stop. Boyd told several people he was trying to listen to hear if the horse and wagon stopped to pick up the woman. As best he could determine from the sound of the solid wheels on the gravel road, he did not hear the buggy stop. Even though he did not believe the vehicle had stopped, as it passed Boyd did his best to look inside. In the extreme dark of this evening he could not tell if the woman was in the convertible top buggy. It was just too dark a night to see clearly inside but it was Boyd's impression that there were two people in the buggy. That was the only vehicle or person that passed Boyd on his lonely two mile walk.

After the brief incident on the bridge, Boyd went on to Greenwich, arriving at 7:25 p.m. When he got to the village Boyd met several people he knew. He asked one of his associates, John Hover, who had also come over the bridge before him, if he had seen the young woman. Hover assured him that had not seen anyone. Hover and Boyd went to the show together. When

51

the performance was over the two men walked back to their homes in Middle Falls. As they passed over the dark bridge, they did not notice lights in any of the windows of the house across the road from where Maggie's body would be found the next day.

Boyd, unlike the other men that testified that day, acknowledged that he had "called on" Maggie. He told the jury that he had called at the house one time taking her for a walk up to the Nolan house and later had walked her back to the Reynolds house. Later in his testimony, Boyd said that the previous summer he had also walked her home from the fair. On each of these occasions the two of them had been alone.

When asked about Maggie's state of mind, Boyd said that, in his opinion, Maggie was generally in "good spirits" and seemed to enjoy life.

With the testimony

of the three single men in the hamlet who were most likely to know and be attracted to Maggie completed, the investigation called on A. M. Crandall, the superintendent of the pulp mill. On the Friday night in question Crandall had left Middle Falls for Greenwich between 7:15 and 7:20 p.m. Crandall, unlike Boyd, had taken a buggy to the village that evening.

As Crandall neared the stone bridge on his way into the village, he saw a woman walking at what appeared to be a regular gait toward Greenwich. Crandall said that he believed the woman to be the one that worked at the Reynolds house. When asked what led him to the conclusion that the woman was Maggie, he answered, "only the impression that any man has on passing someone." This is an interesting comment, since he told of passing several other people on foot that evening but at the hearing he could not recall the identity of any of them.

On the night of Maggie's death Crandall had gone to the Greenwich Hotel for "a while" then returned to Middle Falls, arriving a few minutes after nine. On his way back to Middle Falls he again passed a person who he believed to be the same woman he had passed on his way into Greenwich. The lady was on the Greenwich side of the bridge near Job Sherman's barn. Crandall was certain the time was about 9:00 p.m. as he looked at the clock when he stopped at the hotel in Middle Falls.

Thomas Gettings

was the next single man called. Gettings was present not so much to testify as to his direct knowledge but rather what he had heard relative to the events of October 18th. Gettings related a tale that he had heard from Charles DeGroff. According to Gettings, on that Friday night DeGroff had driven a team into Middle Falls from Greenwich. On his way into the hamlet he had passed two men on the bridge. DeGroff had called out to the men "Hello boys." The two men did not answer. There is no explanation as to why DeGroff was not called to testify directly.

At the time of this investigation there were fewer obstacles to having hearsay evidence admitted into a hearing than exist today. The testimony of Matthew Haren is one of the best examples. Haren was called to confirm a conversation between Will Wilson and himself. White asked Haren if some man, while intoxicated at the Greenwich House, had told him that he knew a very significant point regarding the case and that he (Haren) had related the conversation to Wilson. Haren denied the statements that had been attributed to him through what by now had become a flourishing rumor mill.

On the night of Maggie's death

young Abraham Cipperly, the son of Dr. John Cipperly, was

leading one of his father's horses into the barn when he heard a woman's scream. He guessed the time of the shriek to be at about 7:00 p.m. Abraham judged the outcry to come from just a little ways down the street toward Middle Falls. He thought the sound emanated from in front of Otis Teft's house. This would have put the cry on the road away from Greenwich. The scream, which only lasted a second, sounded to Abraham like it was "choked off." When asked the words in the scream he said that as best the woman called "Oh, don't!" People were troubled about his inaction and when asked if he thought the cry was important enough to check on, he responded, "No sir."

Like the men who had been witnesses before him, Abraham had never seen Maggie in the company of men nor had he seen her out at night alone.

The Washington County Post was, at the time of Maggie's death, the rival local weekly newspaper to *The People's Journal* of Greenwich. *The Post* said that the only important witness of the day was young Abraham Cipperly. They didn't even cover the testimony of the other young men.

Following the testimony
of the men noted above, the hearing was adjourned for another week. Speculation as to what actually occurred that night was running rampant through the rural communities of Washington County. The tales were most pervasive in Greenwich, Cambridge and Middle Falls.

Although the names of the perpetrators had not surfaced, most of the people in the area believed that foul play was responsible for Maggie's death. Those who felt it was murder based their opinion on the scream heard by Cipperly, and the fact that Maggie never walked alone at night. These facts combined with the certainty that she had done all the rest of her

54

chores, such as getting the milk and doing the dishes, was evidence enough to this group that she was in a normal state of mind.

Those in the minority, who still believed the death might have been suicide, based their opinion on Maggie's reported unstable behavior. Their best examples of her instability were the unclean drinking glass and the unmade bread, which were considered as support of the stories about her state of mind told by her friend Julia Nolan.

A second autopsy

on Maggie's body was ordered but by whom is unclear. Five years later Edgar Hull would claim that he had ordered the disinterment, but since he was not even at the hearing that day there is a question as to who felt that a second examination of the body would be appropriate. In any event, Dr. M. Jones of Fort Edward was brought in to perform a second autopsy. This autopsy was held in Cambridge with Drs. Millington, Scott, and Murray again present along with Dr. Niver of Cambridge. Despite pressure from the reporters, none of the doctors gave any indication of their findings prior to the hearing the following Saturday. And there were discoveries made at the examination led by Dr. Jones.

The hearing continued

the following Saturday morning with the testimony of William Dooley being led by District Attorney Hull. Hull had been reelected to his position by the narrowest margin of any of the county officials elected that November. Dooley lived in Middle Falls and on the Friday night Maggie disappeared he had driven his horse over the bridge on the way home from Greenwich. To the best of Dooley's judgement, it was between 9:30 and 10:00 when he drove over the bridge. On the end of the bridge closest to Greenwich, Dooley saw two men dressed in dark clothes, standing facing each other as if engaged in a conversation. Try as hard as he might Dooley was unable to hear what the men were saying. Dooley, like so many others, was struck by how extremely dark it was that night. In his words, "you could not identify anyone at a distance of ten feet." In spite of being pushed by the district attorney, Dooley said he had absolutely no idea of the identity of the two men. Dooley said he had told the story to several people but was only certain of two friends, DeGroff and McGraw.

Dooley's only contribution to the investigation was to support Gettings's observations of the previous week. Gettings had been the first to report that there were two men on the bridge that evening.

Dr. Jones

was brought in as an expert in postmortem examinations. Supported by the observation of four other physicians,   Dr. Jones performed the second autopsy on Maggie's remains. Dr. Jones did a much more thorough examination than his predecessors, with some startling results.

Dr. Jones found a series of marks on Maggie's upper arms. He felt that these marks implied that she had been restrained by severe force. He felt some person had gripped her upper arms with great intensity. With these marks there was, for the first time, a clear indication that Maggie had experienced physical violence prior to her death. The discovery of bruises did not end Dr. Jones's resolve but rather enhanced his desire to be sure of the genesis of her fate.

In feeling the back of Maggie's skull, Dr. Jones came upon a surface wound approximately the size of a quarter dollar. The injury was on the back of Maggie's head near where the skull and backbone come together. His interest peaked as he removed the skin over the mark and found that his suspicions were correct. To Dr. Jones the mark indicated a severe blow had been received on this area of the head. This wound was so grave that it would have caused immediate unconsciousness and perhaps even death.

It was Dr. Jones's opinion, based on further examination of her lungs, heart and blood, that there was clear indication that Maggie's actual death was from asphyxiation, not the head wound. The doctor based his conclusion on the amount of blood in the right side of the heart and the absence of blood in the left side and on the presence of froth in the mouth.

Dr. Jones did not feel that the amount of water in the stomach mattered significantly in determining if the cause was drowning. In Dr. Jones's opinion there were missing pieces for the drowning theory. Specifically there was no mud or sand in Maggie's lungs or trachea. Dr. Jones told the jury that both were common in drowning victims. This was especially true if the person was found in relatively shallow water, as was the case with Maggie. He did point out that the asphyxiation could have occurred either in the water or before her body was placed in the pond.

Dr. Niver, who was present at the autopsy, supported the conclusions of Dr. Jones. When asked if the injury to her head could have happened while she was in the pond, Niver said that the wound was definitely inflicted before the body went in the water.

An attempt was made to clarify
why the head wound had been missed in the first autopsy. Hull had Dr. George Murray recalled. Murray said it was customary to only do an autopsy until the cause of death was determined.

Since there was such a preponderance of evidence that Maggie had drowned, he never considered examining the body further to look for a wound on her head.

Bristol, the undertaker who had laid out Maggie, testified that when her body was in his shop he had not noticed any bruises on her arms. At the time he was responsible for the body, the marks appeared to be merely discolorations not injuries.

To discover Maggie's habits

in the evenings, her best friend, twenty-year-old Julia Nolan, was called to testify. She told the jury of how she and Maggie met almost ever evening to go for a stroll to the post office or would go to their neighbor, Mrs. Sprague's, to listen to her play the piano. Their meetings were usually pre-arranged but sometimes Julia would just call at Maggie's door.

In an effort to protect her friend's reputation, Julia stressed to the jury that Maggie was afraid of the dark and would never walk alone at night.

Julia was asked about how Maggie would dress for their walks. Julia explained that on occasion Maggie would dress up for their walks but usually just wore her working clothes.

There was speculation carried in the newspapers that Maggie may have started out from the Reynolds house alone. For those following this line of reasoning, the motivation was believed to be either impatience in waiting for Julia or perhaps Maggie was going to a secret rendezvous. There was also the possibility that she had changed her plans in the two days since she had seen Julia and had set out for some other venue. The conjecture that she had set off to visit some other home was ceased when Julia testified that the only houses in Middle Falls that she knew of Maggie visiting, other than her own and

Mrs. Sprague's, were those of the Obenaurs, Alwells and Nashes. Other than her visits to those few homes Maggie stayed mostly to herself.

The investigation then went to the issue of Maggie's hair being loose when her body was found in the pond. According to Julia, Maggie always wore her hair up on her head in a roll fastened with a hairpin. Julia went on to explain that when Maggie put her hat on she always put the hairpin through her sacque, not in the hat. This raised the question as to why, if Maggie had committed suicide, had the hatpin been found in the hat and not in the sacque.

Julia contradicted Edmund Boyd's testimony from the previous week. At that time, Boyd said that he had called on Maggie twice. Julia told the jury that he had "called on" Maggie either four or five times.

For those holding to the theory that the death was an act of suicide the next line of questioning proved instant fodder for their conviction. On the Tuesday evening before her death, and on that evening only, Maggie had complained to Julia of not feeling well and told her of seeing Dr. Gray and an Indian doctor. Maggie was so ill that she claimed that she did not feel like going on. The next evening when the two girls went for their walk, Maggie was feeling in her normal high spirits.

Naturally, the jury was curious as to whether Maggie had ever given an indication that she would have considered drowning herself. Julia told them that when Maggie heard the story of how the Widow Patton's husband had taken his own life she told Julia that she could "never do such a thing as that." Their neighbor, Peter Patton, had committed suicide by drowning himself in the Battenkill the previous summer.

Martin Nolan,

Julia's father, told the jury that Maggie was "as nice a girl as ever came into our house." In his opinion she was always lively and was a "girl of good sense."

Seventeen-year-old Willie Teft

was a laborer at the mills, so rather than walk back to his parents in Greenwich he stayed with his grandfather in Middle Falls. On the night Maggie disappeared, Willie was walking from his grandfather's house to the post office when he passed a woman he thought was Maggie. Young Teft was not "very familiar" with Maggie. The woman he saw was walking in the direction of Greenwich (he had passed the woman south of the Reynolds home so she could have just been walking home - not to Greenwich as implied by many later). A little later he passed Boyd in front of Haren's home. In Teft's memory, Boyd was walking in the same direction as Maggie but was behind her.

Mrs. Kate Lansing and Miss Lizzie Grant

were out for a walk that same evening. At 7:00 the two women passed a woman standing alone at the "ordinary crossing." Miss Grant remarked that the woman was   Miss Austin. Mrs. Lansing said no; it was Maggie, Herbert Reynolds housekeeper. Later that night Miss Grant went for a ride into Greenwich with a gentleman friend, who she refused to name. Lizzie told the jury she did not see anyone on the bridge on her way into the village. At 8:30 p.m. Lizzie was on her way back to Middle Falls when she saw a woman standing near the wire fence on the Greenwich side of the bridge.

Rosa Alwell

had been to Thomas Nash's home on two of the occasions when both Maggie and William Scully were there at the same time. William Scully was the first witness and the man who had "saluted" Maggie, as she passed by the week before her death. Although Maggie had never said anything about him, it was Rosa's opinion that Maggie "thought a great deal" of Scully. When questioned about Maggie's health, Rosa said she never complained to her about "any ailments."

Sarah Austin,

the woman Miss Grant thought that she saw that night, was called to determine if she was at the bridge on the night in question. She said that she went to the post office about 8:15 but other than that trip had been home the entire evening. She went on to say that she barely knew Maggie and that the only time Maggie had stopped at the house was when two intoxicated men were on the road to the Reynolds home. On that occasion Sarah's brother had walked Maggie safely home. This story is a clear indication of Maggie's caution and her skill at avoiding a possibly dangerous situation. The story, which was not told by a friend, also is an indication that Maggie had common sense.

Thomas Nash,

who lived in the tenement across the road from where the body was found and the host of Scully, was called but added little to the testimony. He said that the basis for the friendship was between his wife and Maggie. In Nash's recollection, Maggie had visited his home several times but only for short intervals. He said that he never heard Maggie complain about her health or heard her say that she was tired of life.

J. Herbert Reynolds,

Maggie's employer, was the final witness. Herbert's testimony did much to reject some of the comments as to Maggie acting "out of sorts" the night she died. He told the jury that Maggie often left the drinking glasses till the morning, when she would wash them in fresh water. He also confirmed the testimony that Julia and the Obenauer girls had called at the house at the times they had said on the evening Maggie disappeared.

As to the question of whether the Reynoldses knew or cared that Maggie was out, Herbert added that his mother was so worried about Maggie not returning by 9:00 p.m. that she had stayed up until 11:00. Finally his mother had gone to bed assuming Maggie was spending the night with a friend.

After hearing from the witnesses, the coroner's jury deliberated for forty-five minutes before rendering their verdict. Their decision: "That Maggie Horrigan came to her death near the stone bridge between Middle Falls and Greenwich on the evening of the 18th of October 1889, from the effects of an injury upon the back of the head, received before death, from causes unknown and from drowning."

To *The Peoples Journal,* the decision of the coroner's jury was inconclusive. They said that the bruise was an indication of violence while the comments attributed to Maggie by her friends led to equal credibility that Maggie had committed suicide. *The Journal* went on to say that the district attorney, physicians and the police had done everything in their power to determine the cause of Maggie's death. All the other newspapers in the region except *The Whitehall Chronicle* felt that the cause was murder. It is significant to note that the editor and publisher of *The Journal* served as a member of the coroner's jury.

The coroner's jury, because of the second autopsy, had addressed several of the questions regarding Maggie's death. It still left numerous questions unanswered.

Why had so many of the most prominent citizens of Greenwich allowed themselves to be involved in the inquiry into the death of a maid? It could not have been for the money as the men only received a dollar a day from the county for their service.

With the investigation taking over two weeks how had the alleged assailants escaped detection or, at the very least, speculation? Each of the witnesses called, except Boyd, had a concrete alibi. Even the time Boyd could have seen Maggie that evening would have been limited as there were clear times when he was seen first in Middle Falls and later in Greenwich. Were there no people, with the exception of Boyd, who would have a problem explaining their activities that night?

Why were Maggie's hands folded in front of her as if she had been laid out? There is no record that this issue was ever pursued.

Add to these unresolved questions two about the people at the stone bridge. Who was the woman on the bridge early in the evening and who were the two men seen by several people later in the evening?

In the excitement of that night and with the fear of detection, it appears someone knew enough about how to make a death appear to be a suicide to take many strides to hide responsibility for Maggie's death. There is no record that the coroner's jury tried to determine the background required of a potential suspect who would have known enough about the differences between a suicide and a murder to take the steps taken by the assailant(s) that night. This question of knowledge is even more crucial when one considers the extreme pressure the assailant, would have been under that evening.

If the assailants were not from the immediate locale, then they would have needed a buggy to get to and from the scene. This would have meant they had some worth. Why were no men of substance questioned?

If the crime was committed by men from the community, how could they keep their involvement so quiet?

One of the most pressing questions later was, why did Dr. Scott get so involved in the investigation and why would a non-practicing physician be selected to perform an autopsy?

Why was Will Wilson in the room when the autopsy was completed? The man was not a physician or a coroner although he would later describe himself as a coroner's assistant.

In a way, the coroner's jury probably felt that they had done their duty. Yet the outcome left far too many unanswered questions.

Based on the verdict of the coroner's jury, Maggie's death will be called a murder from this point forward.

Despite the desperate wishes of some, the story would not end with the verdict issued by the jury.

The Battle of the Editors

is the only way to describe the series of newspaper reports concerning Maggie's murder that were featured between mid-November of 1889 and January 1890. The coroner's inquest had ended rather ambiguously, with a finding that her death may or may not have been murder. With no real news to report the editors engaged in an exchange of articles that accomplished two objectives. The positive purpose was to develop a theory as to what had happened on that dark October evening. The negative aim was to begin a barrage of slanderous comments toward each other.

The public inquiry had taken over two weeks, yet there was no person charged with a crime, nor was there a leading suspect. There was the unexplained mystery of the injury to the back of Maggie's head, but despite this wound the doctors still believed she died of asphyxiation. As in all cases where there exists an extended gap between the death and the jury's decision, the flow of news and hard evidence had dwindled to a trickle.

The editors of three of the county newspapers compensated for the lack of hard news by engaging in the exchange of public letters that could best be described as the battle of the presses. The editors of these small local newspapers were often the only full-time employees of the periodicals. Despite the obstacles of time and energy, the editors took on this interchange with what appeared to be more zeal than the law officials had for solving the crime.

The attacks made on each other by the editors in the early winter of 1889-90 were often personal. These denunciations were based primarily on whether the editor's newspaper held the position that Maggie was murdered or that she committed suicide.

Essentially, the public conflict was the financial reward of the large number of sales that this form of extremely personal commentary generated. Many readers would buy *The Peoples Journal* on Thursday to see what Morhous had to say about Smart. On Friday these same readers would buy *The Washington County Post* to read Editor Smart's rebuttal or, more often, his censure of Morhous. Because both newspapers were weeklies the patrons had to wait until the following Thursday for the next installment.

On November 8th, the clash began innocently enough when Editor Smart published his opinion as to what happened to Maggie. He explained in detail why it would have been impossible for Maggie to receive the blow to the back of her head and then to fall into the pond. He also did a very good job of questioning how Maggie's clothes were found on one side of the pond and her body the other side. In Smart's opinion, Maggie was murdered and there was no question about that fact. This hard line stand that the death was murder was what aggravated the editors of the rival newspapers. Smart created the beginning of the ghost story when he said, "The rushing sound of the water as it dashes over the rocks and rest in the stillness of the pool will, in the future cause a shudder to pass over all who cross over the bridge as they think of the sad fate of Maggie Horrigan on the night of October 18th, 1889."

The Whitehall Chronicle countered the exchange by carrying a report that strongly supported the concept that Maggie had committed suicide. The grammar of the period sometimes makes reading the articles difficult but they provide a real understanding of the feelings in the communities at the time. The editor, Mr. Teft, was born and raised in Middle Falls. At the time of Maggie's death the Teft family still resided in Middle Falls, which may explain his interest in the case. In his editorial he started by reviewing the exact wording from the coroner's jury. Then he continued:

> The Greenwich people seem to have started out on the theory that she was murdered and instead of having committed suicide and to have adhered to that theory throughout the proceedings in the case. Nothing would satisfy the excited feeling but the establishment of a case of murder.
>
> All the facts brought out by the testimony, seem to us to clearly militate against the theory of murder of violence or tending to show that violence of any kind had been committed, or that there was any motive. The girl was strong, well developed and able bodied: five feet five inches in height and weighing 150 pounds. She was capable of making a stern residence to any one who might attempt an assault on her. Had any one attempted any violence upon her, there would have been some indication of it upon her person or on the spot where it occurred. It would have been impossible to get her over the fence and to the spot where she was found against her will if alive and certainly impossible if she were dead.

The editor then went on to make assertions that were not corroborated by any testimony or document. Where and how he came to his conclusions was unclear, but it should be understood that Teft was a common name around Greenwich and the editor would inevitably have had family in the area. At first blush it can only be assumed that this young editor saw himself as the leader in the new science of psychology:

> She was ordinarily, bright and cheerful but there were times when she was depressed and melancholy. There were times when

she felt life had no charms or attractions for her, and that she had no object worth living for. She had no home to which she could repair; her father not being to her what fathers generally are to their children. There were times when this morbid feeling of loneliness and desolation came over her even in company and she would remark to her associates that she could even wish that she was dead. What must have been this morbid feeling when she was alone, with no one near her to whom she could express her feelings, and no one to cheer and comfort her with a word of sympathy. There was no change in the daily routine of her life from one week and to another, and no prospect of any change. What more natural than, that brooding over her cheerless life in this melancholy manner, the repose of death should seem far preferable and that the dark dale where she went to meet death, so near the thronged highway, and yet so in contrast with it should seem to her the fitting place in which to end her life and relieve herself of its weary burden forever.

To Editor Smart

this report was too much and it was time to fire a volley in defense of Maggie. The editor of *The Post*, based in Cambridge, used his editorial space to attack the behavior of both the people of Greenwich and the editor of *The Whitehall Chronicle*. Although these editorials do not add a lot of facts, there is a lot to be gained regarding the perceptions of the respective communities.

Washington County Post November 15, 1889

One thing is certain, that Maggie Horrigan is dead. Her poor remains have been out and carved and what is left are in St. Patrick's cemetery near this village. WHO IS THE MAN OR MEN OR WOMEN in the case that some citizens of Greenwich are so desirous to protect? If nothing more is to be done, be content with the murderous work of that night, and stop slandering the father of the girl and insulting the intelligence of the community. It is not true that the girl was unkindly treated at her home. It is not true that the doctors all agree that she was drowned; one at least believes that the unfortunate girl was dead some time before her body ever touched the water. We make these remarks because a correspondent of *The Whitehall Chronicle* bases a column article on these two falsehoods, with others of a similar character, for the instruction of an untruth is falsehood as much as a naked lie - worse, for more likely to be deceptive. WHO IS THE PARTY WE REPEAT; that is to be sheltered that so much pain is taken to cover his crime? It is a damn spot that will not out. It is our belief that if the town of Greenwich had exposed iniquitous proceedings in that town of a lascivious nature, this Maggie Horrigan might be alive. The question which suggests itself is this; are a few libertines, through of family good, to smirch the fair fame of so good a township? We unhesitatingly affirm that not a man in Greenwich conversant with the facts believes that the girl committed suicide. We can say to the people of the town that this matter cannot be whistled down the winds. It is only a servant girl – a pretty faced, well formed servant girl. She is dead, let it go. Perhaps some aristocratic brute has caused her death. It is nothing according to the *Chronicle* scribe. We may never know who did the deed, but Washington county is not the county we take it to be if this matter is to end by a cruel slander of John Horrigan – worthy, honest man – to find an excuse for the suicide theory. If the subject was not so painful and so important, one would laugh at the theory that a chaste young maiden, in the bloom of youth, put on her old clothes to commit suicide, and then, afterward, was careful enough to save her hat and jersey. Not a doctor at the autopsy will deny that the wound at the back of her head would have caused almost instantaneous unconsciousness. It is idle to talk. I, on the state of fact show, Maggie Horrigan committed suicide, the case will increase the number of great wonders of the world from seven to eight. It seems to me the writer of the *Chronicle* scribe protests too much. The question GREENWICH PEOPLE should ask themselves is this: Is a girl to be deprived of her life because she would maintain her virtue, and the town's only answer be a slander on the father? The writer of the *Chronicle,* like the fiend or fiends who did the deed, does his work too well.

On November 28th 1889,

Morhous of *The People's Journal* felt compelled to respond to Smart's editorial published two weeks before. We look now to the context of the editorial not the logic. Morhous said of Smart's editorial, "at first we thought to omit all notice of those unwarranted and wild ravings of some unnatural mind;" As if an unnatural mind is not enough of an attack Morhous went on to make the attack truly personal: "…it seems best to assume, as most do, that the writer was a little worse for wear; that the cravings of his stomach had been answered with water simply, which could not sustain his mind, accustomed to the aid of more powerful liquid incentives."

Morhous explained that his paper had not tried to cover for anyone. He pointed out correctly that no names had yet been put forward that had not been checked by detectives. For the next several paragraphs Morhous went on to stress that Maggie's death, unless they could prove it was murder, was better left a suicide.

Morhous put forward a statement that was simply not supported even by the testimony reported in his own newspaper. He said that all the doctors agreed that Maggie was alive when she entered the water. The doctors' testimony in fact questioned the drowning based on the lack of water in her lungs and stomach. The doctors said she died of asphyxiation, not drowning.

In this same edition of *The Journal* was an article originally printed in *The Chronicle* that supported the logic of its original article that Maggie's death was by suicide.

The next day

Smart was on the attack. He focused on his fellow editor "brother Teft." Smart made his point very clear when he said of Teft's last editorial, "your last article was mainly bosh." Smart took neither the highroad nor low-road telling Teft his business:

> As a newspaper man he should state the facts accurately, as a lawyer he should make sure that he had the evidence not manufactured it, as a psychologist he should turn his attention to some of the residents of the locality where this murder was committed.

On December 6th,

Smart responded to the charge that he drank by "conceding this to be the fact." He went on to assault his adversary at *The Journal* by calling him "one so ignorant as you." And pointing out that "as you grow older my young friend you will learn that personal abuse of one's opponent is only a confession of weakness."

The battle peaked

on December 12th, when Morhous made the following comment on one of Smart's editorials in which Smart called Morhous his young friend: "It is plain that not a sense of decency, nor any good impulse saved the 'young friend.'" Not satisfied with this attack, Morhous continued later with comments about Smart being a liar. "Your conceded uncommon natural ability in that respect, improved and developed by assiduous cultivation during a long career, would deter most any one from a lying contest with you." *The Journal* closed the article with a challenge to Smart to provide the names of people from Greenwich who he felt were either withholding evidence or were involved in the actual attack on Maggie.

On December 13th

Smart shifted his attack from the editor to be more direct at the rumors that were floating around. He called upon *The Journal* to provide the name of the doctor who had supposedly tried to minister to Maggie for several hours the night of her attack. It is apparent from this report that rumors were already beginning that there was some doctor involved. The editorial went on to point out that there existed an element that wanted to see two "dissipated brothers" (not named but the description matches the Durlings who will be discussed later) charged for her death when according to Smart, they had a perfect alibi. According to Smart, "There are ugly facts about this case which show the workings of an undercurrent of influence aimed at hiding and covering up and thwarting the citizens of Greenwich who have honestly and diligently to detect the perpetrator of the crime."

For some reason *The Journal* did not respond to Smart in their December 19th edition.

By December 20th,

Smart had waited patiently for a week before he responded on the personal level. In the meantime Governor Hill had provoked the county to offer a reward of $1,000. Smart made his comments in two places. In one he said about the reward, "Can this crime be smothered much longer?" In the next sentence he threw the gauntlet back at Morhous with, "Tell us what you know about this murder, not what you know about any editorial scribbler."

Smart went on to quote people from Greenwich who admitted that on the night of Maggie's death they could not have identified family members at a distance of ten feet. This was actually a good move on Smart's part as he quoted people from *The Journal's* base and it called into question the testimony of people who said they had seen Maggie at a distance of twelve to fifteen feet.

Smart did not drop the attack on *The Journal.* After commenting on how *The Journal* had not run a single article about the murder, he went on to say:

> Come now, in all fairness, skipping the question of what the editor of the Post does or drinks, tell us who killed MAGGIE HORRIGAN? The question as to the follies of youth of middle age as between us can be settled afterwards, but assist, as we hope you will, and are half inclined to think you can, to discover the men and women, either or both, who were the parties to the murder of this innocent, virtuous girl.

In early January the public inquiry resumed. The reintroduction of evidence seemed to settle but not quiet the editors whose personal vendetta would not soon pass.

H. C. Morhous

Mary McMaster

Dr. S. W. Scott

Edgar Hull

James White

The Reynolds home

The Greenwich House

The houses' of LaVake and Brooks on Church Street Greenwich

Edgar Hull's house in Fort Edward

The Second Inquiry

began on January 9th, 1890, nearly three months after Maggie's murder. The forces that compelled District Attorney Hull to call for an official re-opening of the public investigation into Maggie's death were the editorials in the local newspapers and the numerous rumors running rampant throughout the county. The editorials that argued Maggie's death was a murder, especially those from   Mr. Smart, of *The Post*, gave rise to a public outcry for the truth. The editorials that held the death was a suicide, which were carried in *The Journal* and *The Chronicle,* did little to stifle the community's demand for an answer as to what had befallen Maggie.

Although not intentional at the onset, this second investigation was broken into three distinct parts. Each part was two days long. The first, which accomplished little except to exonerate some suspects, was in January. The second part began in the first week of February. This part was preceded by some startling events. This portion of the inquiry would have caused Maggie's spirit to think peace was finally at hand. The third and final portion of the inquiry was in late March.

The January 1890 examination was considered by Hull to be a grand jury although no jury is ever named. The inquiry was held in Middle Falls before Maggie's former neighbor, Justice Henry Mansfield. Since there was nothing that resembled a courtroom in the hamlet the hearing was held in the home of A. T. Sprague. Sprague, who also ran the post office in Middle Falls, was Mansfield's son-in-law. For reasons not stated District Attorney Edgar Hull was not present but had again left James White in charge of the examination. White was the lawyer from Greenwich who substituted for Hull in November. In point of fact, Hull had not been present since the opening portion of the investigation. Hull's most important contribution to the first inquiry was when he ordered that Maggie's remains be exhumed and a second autopsy be performed.

The November coroner's jury had focused on the cause of Maggie's death with a peripheral inquiry into who may have been responsible. The examination that opened in January went further than its predecessor in trying to determine who was accountable for Maggie's death. To accomplish its mission, this inquiry first tried to establish Maggie's normal pattern and her behavior the night of her death. The inquiry also tried to establish a motive and accessibility to Maggie. To establish all that required calling numerous people to the stand. Among those called to testify were the entire Reynolds family, Maggie's friends and associates, and others who had been out on the street the evening she disappeared.

There was a series of rumors afloat that needed to be addressed or the case would have the entire community at odds with itself. The first rumor was that Herbert Reynolds was somehow responsible for Maggie's death. The second placed the blame on Maggie's only known suitor, Ed Boyd. The third rumor was that a wrench had been found that had human hair attached. The assumption was that the wrench was the murder weapon. The last rumor was that Dr. Scott had left the theater the night of Maggie's death. It was hypothesized that he had been called upon by Maggie's assailant(s) to treat her for the head wound.

Christine Parker

was the first witness in the second investigation. Ms. Parker ran a small grocery in Middle Falls across the highway from the Cowan Hotel; her husband was one of the hamlet's blacksmiths. As was her daily custom, Maggie had gone to Parker's grocery on the evening she was murdered to procure milk. Since Maggie came every night, if Mrs. Parker had something else to do she would leave a pail of milk on the side steps on the west side of her house. Upon finding the fresh pail of milk Maggie would take it and leave the empty one from the previous night in exchange. Mrs. Parker told Mansfield that on occasion Maggie would have one of her girlfriends with her when she came for the milk. This would have been on their evening stroll. On the night in question, Mrs. Parker had been resting on a couch across from the window. She heard someone come for milk between 6:30 and 7:00 p.m. She did not see the person but assumed it was Maggie. To Mrs. Parker there was nothing distinctive about that night. Her testimony about her memory of what occurred the night of the incident is probably as accurate as possible, since who among us can remember what we were doing on any given evening four months before.

Mrs. Mary McMaster,

a house guest in the Reynolds home, was the second witness, her daughter, Mary Lena, the third witness. Herbert was the fourth witness. The two McMaster women supported each other's testimony in every detail. They went into great detail in the arrangement of the rooms in the house and where each person was during the afternoon and evening. The intent of this line of questioning was threefold. White was trying to determine if Maggie could have gone to her room without anyone noticing. White's theory was that if she could have gone to her room, this could have placed the time of death later – it was clearly established that she could not have gone to her room without someone in the family seeing her.

Second, he was trying to establish where in the house Herbert Reynolds was during the evening. As a single man familiar with Maggie, Herbert's name had been bantered around as a possible suspect. To White's dismay, Herbert was accounted for the entire evening.

White was also trying to ascertain if Maggie's routine was somehow broken. An abandoned habit would imply that she was confused and would support the theory of her death being a suicide.

In Mary and Lena's judgement, Maggie's daily chores were accomplished as usual. Even though they were guests, the two were in a position to make such a determination as they were in the habit of staying at Herbert Reynolds's home for a few days approximately every three weeks.

Substitute attorney White was fixated on how Maggie had gotten her hat and shawl. Everyone agreed that Maggie normally kept her outerwear in her room until she went for her evening walk. It had already been established that the only place in the house where Maggie had been that evening was in the kitchen. The McMaster women could not say how Maggie got her hat or shawl on the night in question but did not think that it was important. For all they knew Maggie may have had her outwear in the kitchen all day.

Mary's description of the house indicated that Maggie's room was upstairs. The stairs were off of her brother's library. After dinner the Reynolds women had all adjourned to the parlor. Herbert had gone into his library, which was between the parlor and the dining room. The servants stairway was off the library so Maggie could not have gotten to her room without going past Herbert. The entire Reynolds family would all say that Maggie never went upstairs that night.

Herbert Reynolds
had more at stake than the other witnesses did when he took his

place on the stand. His proximity to the victim, combined with his being single, made him one of the prime targets of the investigation. Before the case would finally be over, Herbert would actually be accused of Maggie's death by some of the newspapers. There were two different theories as to what Herbert did to Maggie that caused her death. Both theories included the injury found on the back of her head. In one theory it was professed that when she rejected him he hit her from behind with the intent of taking advantage of her. The second theory is not much different except that it had the two in a frontal assault with Maggie falling back against the wood stove as she fought to protect her virtue. Through his own and the testimony of his family, it was evident that Herbert Reynolds was not involved in Maggie's death. This hearing had provided him with the opportunity to clear his name.

Counselor James White then shifted his focus to Ed Boyd. To get to the issue of whether Ed had walked Maggie to the bridge White called on Julia Nolan, Willie Teft, Sarah Austin and her mother, the Obenauer sisters, Kate Lansing and Ed Boyd, himself.

The testimony in this portion
of the investigation was a lot of "he said, she said" revolving around theories that the above people felt. The best example was when Mrs. Austin was said to have been telling others that she had seen Maggie walking toward Greenwich in the company of a mechanic – which would be Ed Boyd. Although Julia Nolan said on the stand that she had heard Mrs. Austin was making the statement,   Mrs. Austin denied that she had ever made such comments.

What was learned from all the banter was that young Teft and Kate Lansing both saw Maggie that evening while she was walking with the milk. Miss Lansing was less clear about what she had seen, implying that she may have seen Maggie later walking toward the bridge. Lansing, however, lacked credibility, as she would not name the man she was supposedly with that night. She did say that after the walk with her mystery man, her friend had left her on the street to go to Greenwich by buggy.

Maggie's close friends

did not change their reports about her behavior or her habits. Will Teft added little to what he had said in November. It was his memory that when he was walking into Middle Falls he first passed Maggie then Ed Boyd. When Ed Boyd took the stand the issue for him was to establish finally that he did not catch up to Maggie. The reporters, and others in the room when Boyd testified, were reasonably certain that Maggie was far enough ahead of Boyd that she had gotten back into the Reynolds house before he passed. By the time Boyd passed the house, Maggie was inside putting away the milk.

The identity of the woman Ed Boyd said he passed on the bridge that night remained in question.

The next day

began with the denial of admission to the hearing of all the reporters. Attorney White announced that District Attorney Hull had notified him that reporters were not to be permitted in the hearing room. Hull cited as a reason that several witnesses had complained about being misrepresented in the newspapers. Hull used as his authority a point in the law that allowed grand juries to be held without a public audience. There were two problems with using the law as Hull did on this occasion. First, the hearing in Middle Falls was not a grand jury. The second problem was that non-reporters were permitted into the room.

The Troy Times immediately found a person who had attended the hearings from the beginning to sit in the room and relate what occurred to their reporter. Hull, as we shall see later may have had an ulterior motive for restricting the ability to accurately report the testimony being given.

One of the reporters who was waiting outside happened to have two interesting conversations to report. He ran into an interested spectator who desired to be quoted. John Horrigan, Maggie's father, was at the hearing that morning. He told the reporter of Maggie's state of mind and how she never would have considered suicide. To this caring father, a beautiful loving daughter had been lost, and worse yet there was what he felt was a conspiracy to make her death appear a suicide. If this rumor were to stand she would have lost her life and her reputation.

The other person was standing outside, rejoicing in the exclusion of the reporters. This unnamed man came over to the reporter to inform him that there was no story and that he should just go home. The reporter asked him how he was so sure that the death was a suicide. The man said, "because Dr. Scott says it is."

Testimony on January 10th

began with Horace Salisbury. Horace Salisbury maintained a hotel on the southern end of Middle Falls. Salisbury was at least as famous for the whiskey he brewed as he was as an innkeeper. He had recently paid a seventy-five-dollar fine for the sale of illegal alcohol. According to Salisbury, on the Monday after Maggie's death he traded Al Durling two glasses of cider for a wrench. Al Durling was one of those characters who lived life on the edge. When Salisbury looked at the wrench the next morning he noticed that it had what appeared to be the red hair of a human stuck to it. He placed the wrench in newspaper and locked it in a bureau. Over the next few weeks he only took the wrench out to show it to his wife and "one or two intimate friends." Eventually, Salisbury took the wrench to one of the most respected physicians in the area, Dr. Gray. After a microscopic examination, Gray told Salisbury that his assumption was correct and that the hair was from a human.

Salisbury's testimony satisfied neither those who felt the wrench was a weapon nor those who felt it was not the weapon. The red hair was a strong indication that it may have been used to strike Maggie. Since this was long before DNA evidence there was no way to directly link the wrench and Maggie's death. The question of the source of the injury to Maggie's head remained open. It should be pointed out that it was a time of gravel roads and stress on wagons, everyone traveled with a set of tools to make any necessary repairs.

Mrs. Henry "Mat" Heath,

about whom much more would be put forward later, was then called to the stand. Heath had a house between the Reynolds house and Greenwich. The Heath house did "not have a very good reputation." Heath told the court she was laying down on her couch and had no idea if Maggie had passed her house that evening. When asked if there were any strangers in the area that night, Mrs. Heath responded in a gruff voice that she had no idea if there were any men "in the vicinity that night."

John Mulligan

was the last witness that morning. Mulligan shifted the focus of the inquiry to the actions of Dr. Scott. It needs to be noted that John Mulligan was a cousin of Maggie's. Mulligan was at Scott's office at the Greenwich Hotel the night Maggie died.

John told the justice that he saw a man come in and whisper to Dr. Scott. Scott immediately called for his team. According to Mulligan when Dr. Scott was informed that the wagon had just been cleaned he said it made no difference because he needed to go to Middle Falls "at once." When asked, Mulligan could not say for certain if Dr. Scott actually left for Middle Falls that night or not.

A break was taken

so that those conducting the session could have lunch. In the early afternoon Dr. Scott took the stand. Dr. Scott was a deliberate man, as evidenced by how carefully his words were selected. He told the justice that he was not certain if he ever saw "Maggie Horrigan previous to her death." This left him the option of later having a recollection of her alive. According to Dr. Scott he had lent his Cortland buggy to Ed Barber, a notorious drinking man, the evening of October 18th. To Dr. Scott, the issue of his involvement was closed. For him the matter was simple. He had established that he did not have access to his buggy on the night in question; therefore, he could not have gone to Middle Falls. The unstated implication was that without transportation he could not have treated Maggie.

Unlike Herbert Reynolds, who was essentially exonerated by the testimony at this hearing, the rumor that Dr. Scott was somehow involved would not die with his deposition.

Tena Alderman,

a local girl who worked in the shirt factory in Greenwich, was the next witness. Tena Alderman lived with her parents on the road to Argyle. On the night Maggie was killed Tena had walked home over the stone bridge at a little after 6:00 p.m. Between October and the reconvening of this hearing, Tena had, on at least one occasion, stopped and visited with the notorious

Mrs. Heath. While talking with Mrs. Heath, Tena related how on the evening of the murder she had seen a man walking back and forth in front of Mrs. Heath's house. Mrs. Heath had related that the person was a crazy man named Frank Green. For reasons never explored, Mrs. Heath urged her strongly not to tell anyone about having seen Green. With Mat Heath's reputation there was probably a link between Green and herself – which may have had nothing to do with Maggie - that she did not want to explain. Subsequently, Mrs. Heath and Tena had had a falling out over whether Tena had said that Mrs. Heath "could throw light" on the subject of Maggie's death. At the time of Tena's testimony, the two women were no longer speaking to each other.

For no apparent reason

the last Reynolds family member in the area, Herbert and Mary's brother, Pitt, was called. All he really presented was that he was not at the house that evening.

In one last desperate effort to make it appear that Maggie was in a state of depression, Mrs. Josephine Sprague, whose home the hearing was conducted in, was called. In addition to being the host of the hearing, Mrs. Sprague's husband was the postmaster and she was usually present each evening when people came to pick up their mail. According to Josephine, on the Wednesday before her death, Maggie had looked disappointed when she noticed there was no mail for her.

The hearing was adjourned

until February 6th. Two days had been spent on the interviews with little new information coming to light. The only winners were the members of the Reynolds family, all of whom were absolved of any involvement. Ed Boyd was also in better standing, as it was ultimately believed that he did not see

Maggie that evening. The rumor that Dr. Scott may have more knowledge than he was sharing and may have in fact treated Maggie that night was still circulating. There was also the matter of the wrench with red hairs on it.

The two days of the hearing left the communities of Greenwich and Middle Falls with a shared sense of frustration. There were two distinct factions. One side continued to hold the death a suicide. This group was the minority, but it was by far the more verbal clique. Like the man outside the hearing, those who supported the suicide theory, on occasion, stated that their allegiance was to   Dr. Scott. The other side, those who felt the death was murder, was sure that the truth was being withheld. The major problem that this group had was they could not agree on specific suspects but instead allowed rumors that named just about everyone to dominate the case.

The rumors about the perpetrators fell into three categories. The first was that the perpetrators were from the lower end of the social spectrum. The second was that those involved were the sons and friends of the wealthy end of the community. The third, and by far the smallest, was that those involved were from outside the immediate area.

A major break
happened just two days before the case was scheduled to reconvene. After a circuitous chase around northern Rennsselaer County and southern Washington County the police were able to arrest fourteen-year-old Edward Scully.

Scully was the character in this story on which many hang their opinion as to whether Maggie was murdered or committed suicide. His importance is interesting since both sides use quotes from this undisciplined young lad to support their position. His importance is especially interesting since Scully was also probably one of the least trustworthy figures involved in the inquiry into Maggie's death. There was no blood relationship between Edward Scully and William Scully, the man that stayed with the Nash family and was considered by Maggie to be interesting.

On February 4th, Deputy Sheriff Gray along with Detective Price arrested Edward Scully in Eagle Bridge, a community near the Vermont border. The official charges on which he was held related to a stolen coat. Scully was really being held to determine what information he had concerning the murder of Maggie Horrigan.

Despite his youth, Scully was well known to the police, having already served eighteen months in a reformatory for horse theft and burglary. Like all who have been convicted, Scully considered the charges unfair. In Scully's side of the story, he had borrowed a cousin's horse and had permission to be driving the animal. He would admit that he had driven the animal too fast for a hot day. According to Scully, the real problem was the animal's care subsequent to his returning the animal to his cousin. Scully told anyone who questioned him about the incident that when the horse was returned his cousin had fed and watered him too much while the animal was still heated. Scully would contend that it was the care that caused the horse to become sick not his running it in the heat. In any event, the horse was lame for some time and his cousin had issued a warrant for Scully's arrest.

In 1889-90, because of what Scully considered problems with the law, he actively stayed away from Greenwich. His long-term avoidance was despite the fact his parents resided in the village.

From the first inclinations that there was a link between Scully and Maggie's death, the police did not believe that he was a principal in the murder, but rather had somehow attained some special knowledge regarding the matter. Several of the better investigative reporters soon learned that, since the beginning of December, many of the rumors about Maggie's death could be traced directly or indirectly to stories being told by Scully. The question was did the stories originate with Scully or was he just retelling them.

After having spent two months bragging that he had information concerning Maggie's death, it was time for the police to step in and find out just how much Scully could help in resolving the issues.

The night prior to his arrest, Scully was drunk at a tavern in Eagle Bridge. In the course of his binge, he told several people that he knew all about Maggie's murder. More important than just the story being told by Scully was the support that was given to the way he had attained the information he was telling. That evening Scully told several of the men at the bar that he was in the habit of sleeping in the barn near where Maggie's body had been found. The barn in question was owned by Job Sherman, an attorney in Greenwich.

Following his arrest, there was a report in most of the newspapers that "it is said that some time ago a resident of Greenwich, to whom Scully had told some of what he knew, offered him a liberal sum [$500 was the figure usually bantered about] to swear out a warrant against a certain man." The reports in two newspapers went further, saying the man for whom the warrant was to be issued was Dr. Scott, the man who was originally placed on the coroner's jury then later headed the first autopsy.

Three weeks before Scully's arrest Detective Price had become actively involved in the investigation. Price worked for the Pinkerton Agency and was assigned to the Troy office. In the Victorian Era, most police agencies did not have their own detective bureau. In the late 1860s, Pinkerton, who had become famous for his intelligence work during the Civil War, opened a private detective business to supply services to local law enforcement agencies on an as needed basis. When not employed by a police force, the Pinkerton agents would work independently on various investigations that offered a reward.

There were several problems with this structure. The motivation for entering an inquiry became financial, not the search for justice. The Pinkerton detectives would only get involved if the potential financial rewards warranted their efforts. Many poor criminals who committed petty crimes were pleased with the policy. Since the crimes these offenders committed were often against each other there was limited monetary reward. Therefore, they did not have to worry about a professional detective engaging in the investigation. The second major problem was the policy of the Pinkerton Agency. Under the company's rules all records were kept sealed. That meant that much of the background information and the information that exonerated some suspects from further scrutiny were not revealed.

Price's reasons

for being engaged in this case are unclear. The sheriff or district attorney may have employed him or he could have been working for the reward. Although Hull would later write a letter implying that he had engaged Price, in reality, it appears his motive was a reward. There are several financial records in the county archives concerning costs in this trial, but there are none that indicate that the Pinkerton Agency was paid for a private investigation into Maggie's death.

In December 1889, New York State Governor Hill had pressured the Washington County sheriff into offering a reward for information leading to an arrest and conviction of Maggie's killer(s). Not wanting to use the county's money the sheriff had the reward backed by some of the citizens of Greenwich. Several of those involved in offering to support the reward had been on the coroner's jury. One of those offering to pay for information was Henry C. Morhous, the editor of *The Peoples Journal*. This was the same man who was adamant in his columns that Maggie had committed suicide. It would appear that his support of the reward was more of a political decision than a belief that he would have to actually pay a portion of the expense.

Tracking Scully

led the officers in a big circle as they tried to make the arrest. Since Scully had no address the two officers had to start by checking his last known hangouts. Armed with the warrant, the officers went first to Cambridge. Not finding Scully in the village, the officers hired a buggy and spent the rest of the day in search of the young knave. Their trek took them to the hamlets of Lansingburgh, Spiegletown, Schaghticoke, Johnsonville, and finally Eagle Bridge.

Even when Detective Price and Deputy Sheriff Everett Gray came to Eagle Bridge Scully still tried to avoid capture. The officers entered a bar in the hotel and asked if Scully had been seen there. The response was negative and the officers left after giving the site a visual inspection. As Price was walking down the street he had a sensation that the bartender was not telling the truth regarding Scully's presence. Price stopped and watched the door for a minute. Moments later, Price's intuition was rewarded. As he had suspected, Scully was secreted somewhere in the bar. As Price stood across the street, Scully tried to slip out the front door. Price and Gray immediately arrested Scully without any resistance. At the time of his arrest Scully had on a stolen coat with $.50 and four baggage claim tickets in his pocket. It was determined that Scully had stolen the coat from a barn where he had slept the previous Sunday night. The stolen coat supported the belief that Scully was in the habit of staying in barns. When he was in the Greenwich neighborhood it is suspected that he stayed in Sherman's barn.

After Detective Price and Deputy Gray arrested Scully, they took him back to Troy to await his testimony on the opening day of the investigation. It was lucky for the two officers that they had arrested Scully when they did. On the trip to Troy he told them he had had plans to leave the next day for North Adams, Massachusetts, via Bennington, Vermont. He even claimed that there was a man in Eagle Bridge who was preparing a wagon to take him to Vermont as the officers were placing him under arrest.

After his arrest, the officers had Scully sequestered in the Troy jail. The isolation was to assure that no one could get a statement from him prior to his testimony in the upcoming inquiry. The two officers were so serious about their not being any questions asked by Troy's investigative reporters that Gray went home to Johnsonville on the next available train, while Price registered in a local hotel under another name.

At the time of his arrest

Scully told the officers he had not been in Greenwich since the previous September 14th. As soon as Scully's story was printed in the regional newspapers, other persons started placing him in the community several times since that date. The question of his presence was only the first of many times Scully's various tales would be countered by others.

Henry Cipperly

was one of the persons that could place Scully in the vicinity of Middle Falls on the night that Maggie died. Cipperly, whose nephew Abraham had heard a woman cry out the night of Maggie's death, had given Scully a ride from Easton to Melville the morning Maggie's body was found. On that ride Scully had told Cipperly how he had spent the previous night in a barn.

Rumors and speculation

started the day Maggie's body was discovered. Beginning in December reports had started to spread throughout the region that Maggie had been abducted with the intent of either a robbery or rape and that her death was an "accidental murder," not deliberate. As in all spectacular cases involving the death of a beautiful young woman it is only natural that consideration is given to a motive of either attempted rape or revenge. The speculation that these were the intents of those who caused Maggie's misfortune was almost immediate. What was added to the reports that started to be published in December was detail. Specifically, that when she was grabbed, she had resisted.

Maggie was a strong girl - far stronger than her assailants had expected. She was used to doing laundry by hand and hauling the family's water in large pails. In the reports, her resistance was more than the assailants anticipated. To quiet her, they hit her on the head. The stories said that while she was unconscious Maggie's assailants had taken her to a barn. Realizing that their limited plan had gone astray, the men felt compelled to find medical help. Many of these stories, in varying degrees, could be traced to Edward Scully.

Four weeks before his arrest

Scully had been visiting in the hamlet of Buskirk in northern Rensselear County. Hungry and looking for a free meal, Scully called at the door of the large white house with a copula, near the church. Scully later tried to deny he was ever at the house in question. The house would later be described in great detail as evidence that he had, in fact, had dinner there. The house in question was the property of Mrs. Emma Ecyclesymer. Mrs. Ecyclesymer was a kind-hearted person unable to ignore the plaintive looks of the thin young man in front of her that day. She invited Edward in to the kitchen for supper. Her married daughter waited in the dining room and listened through the open door to the conversation that ensued.

As Mrs. Ecyclesymer served a simple meal, she asked Scully where he was from. She would later claim that she was concerned that Scully might have recently run away from his home and she wanted to be sure his parents were aware of his location. With the instant, if not truthful, answers for which he would become known, Scully responded that he was living in Troy but he was originally from Greenwich. It was only natural that Emma asked him what he knew about the Greenwich Mystery (the name often used in the newspapers for the story of Maggie's death). Scully proceeded to tell his hostess that he knew all about the case. He went on to say that he knew Maggie "as well as he knew anybody." This he attributed to a supposed engagement of his older brother to Maggie. Edward Scully did not have an older brother. It would have been probable that Edward may have tried to twist the relationship of the surname he shared with William Scully, the first person called to testify and the man on whom Maggie may have had a crush.

Either seeking gossip or as a challenge to his bold statement, Mrs. Ecyclesymer asked Scully to tell her what he knew of the case. Scully told his benefactor a complete tale. It began when two men picked up Maggie in a carriage almost exactly in front of the Reynolds house. Scully said the men picked her up when she was going to get the milk. Scully was so detailed that he said that the coins needed to pay for the milk and the pitcher had been found on the Reynolds lawn. He even told how the pitcher was broken. According to Scully's story, when Maggie had continued to struggle even when they held her arms and a hand over her mouth, one of the men had hit her over the head with the butt end of a whip. This explained the mark on the back of her head.

Over his supper, Scully went on to relate how when the men realized that she was seriously injured they had taken Maggie to Sherman's barn. The barn in question was near the pond where her body was found the next day. The men had parked their carriage under the attached shed and carried Maggie inside. After the two had a conversation as to what they should do, it was agreed that they would seek medical assistance. Scully told Mrs. Ecyclesymer that the physician they selected was Dr. Scott. Scully went on to say that in the dark barn, Dr. Scott "worked on" the unconscious Maggie for over three hours, trying all that he could imagine to bring the limp girl back to consciousness. When Dr. Scott finally accepted that he could not help, he told her assailants, "they could do what they pleased with their victim, he would not give them away." Scully told Mrs. Ecyclesymer that after the doctor gave up on Maggie and drove away, the assailants shoved her body through a back window in the barn and carried her down to the pond where they threw her in.

Naturally curious,
Mrs. Ecyclesymer asked how he became aware of what had

happened. There were two responses attributed to Scully. In one he told his host that he was first aware of what happened when he found blood on the floor of the barn the next day. The second tale had him asleep in the loft of the barn when he overheard the events below.

In either case, those who held that his story was fabricated pointed to the fact that the head wound had not resulted in blood, therefore how could Scully have found blood the next morning? The lack of a bleeding wound and the extreme darkness of the night were support enough for those who wanted to dismiss Scully's testimony and stay with the suicide theory. They forgot that Maggie also had cuts on two of her fingers. The suicide advocates also pointed out that the pitcher was not found on the front lawn, as was stated in part of Scully's story.

Those who wanted to believe Scully, pointed to the window in the back of the barn and the path down to the pond - the site where Maggie's body was found. They further supported their argument with the issue of time. Scully's story matched the time element that was noted in the autopsy. Scully's story also explained why her hair was down – from the attempted treatment by Dr. Scott.

There are weaknesses in Scully's story. First, how would the men have known of Dr. Scott unless they were local? Second, if there were only two men involved, would they both have left her to look for a doctor? Even if she were unconscious, would they not have left someone with her in case she awoke?

The day after his arrest, Scully was taken by train from Troy to Middle Falls where he was to testify as to his knowledge of the events relating to the death of Maggie Horrigan. As the first witness in this portion of the inquiry, young Scully testified that he had never told any story regarding Maggie and knew nothing of her death.

On the second day of the hearing, Mrs. Ecyclesymer and her daughter Mrs. Brownell both testified as to what had happened when Scully had supper at their house. The two women added two other details to the story previously attributed to Scully. In their testimony the women noted that when Scully was asked if the men who committed the act were Irish he had said, "No, an Irishman would not do such a mean thing." Mrs. Ecyclesymer had asked the boy if the men were rich or poor. The women both testified that he responded "they weren't poor."

In an effort to clarify who was being untruthful, Scully was brought in to face Mrs. Ecyclesymer. He denied ever seeing the woman before. With the gentle lead of a grandmother, Mrs. Ecyclesymer reminded the young man of the meal and her house. Again he denied knowing the woman. Eventually Scully admitted that he may have said the things Mrs. Ecyclesymer attributed to him but that if he did it was just a tale. Although not everyone believed Scully, there was a pervasive sentiment that the young boy had somehow been intimidated into not testifying.

It would be a week

before it was learned that Wilson, the man who
- helped take Maggie's body out of the pond,
- had helped carry Maggie's body to the wagon
- worked part time for Dr. Scott and
- had mysteriously been present at the first autopsy,

had met the train that brought Scully to Middle Falls and was alone with him for several minutes.

If what Scully had told Mrs. Ecyclesymer was made up,

he had developed a story that synthesized the rumors that were flying around the county.

Suddenly the memories

of several others had been jarred by the story told by Scully. Some of the other witnesses at this inquiry added testimony that would support portions of what Scully had told Mrs. Ecyclesymer.

One witness whose memory was awakened was James St. Mary. St. Mary lived on a farm a mile and a half from Greenwich. His farm was on a road perpendicular to the road into Greenwich. At about 8:00 p.m. on the night of the show, St. Mary and his wife drove into town. As they drove their wagon into the village, they heard a woman cry out. They were about at the Heath house at the time. St. Mary told Justice Mansfield that he stopped his wagon to determine the location of the sound. While his wagon was stopped he could hear the sounds of a second wagon driving rapidly up the crossroads near the bridge. The outcry was not repeated but it was his belief that the sound had come from between where he had stopped and the village. It was only speculation, but St. Mary thought the sound came from the other wagon. The time of St. Mary's departure is suspicious. According to the newspaper reports he didn't leave for the show until a half-hour after it began. It is very likely that the times should be adjusted back one hour.

Mrs. Noah Remington lived in Middle Falls in a house near the junction of the road to Argyle. Like so many others, shortly before 7:00 p.m. on the night Maggie was murdered, Mrs. Remington had started on her walk to the post office. Mrs. Remington contributed three suspicious occurrences to the story. As Mrs. Remington passed the Reynolds house a team of horses started up suddenly. It was her belief that the team came from the Reynolds house. Mrs. Remington also passed a man with a lantern leading a horse. Second she met a man on the street with a light overcoat and stiff hat. Since the reporters were banned form the proceedings it is unclear the order of these events. Mrs. Remington would have had to pass the Reynolds house both on her way to the post office and her way back home. On which trip the team pulled out is not in the record. Mrs. Remington's testimony with respect to Edmond Boyd does tend to eliminate him as a suspect as he would not have had time to catch up to Maggie that night.

Looking for suspects

on the lower end of the social spectrum remained one of the themes of this investigation. There was also a concerted effort by the press and possibly the public to link Dr. Scott to the incident.

For those looking for perpetrators with an arrest record the Durling brothers, Alfred and Palmer (Parm), seemed to fit the bill. In the area the name Palmer is often pronounced with two R's - Parmer. It is from this pronunciation that Palmer Durling received his nickname, Parm. Mrs. Heath, who along with her two sons had a house between the Reynolds house and the place where Maggie's body was found, also became a focus of rumors. Combine these two groups with Horace Salisbury who, at the time of Maggie's murder, was charged with violations of the excise laws, and you have a neighborhood ripe with mistrust and suspects.

The Durlings had been born in a rural community in Pennsylvania. Prior to the Civil War the family moved to Washington County. The family lived in the town of Easton just across the covered bridge from Middle Falls. Their lives were basic tragedies. Alfred Durling and his wife had lost several children. Palmer had been to jail and during the period between Maggie's murder and this inquiry was convicted of robbing geese from a local farmer and was again sent to the county jail.

With Palmer Durling in jail, there was only his brother, Alfred, to question. Alfred claimed that on the night Maggie was murdered he and his brother left Salisbury's at 6:00 p.m. Alfred maintained that they then went straight home. Unfortunately, the only witness Alfred had was his wife.

There is a real question as to what weight should be given to any of Durling's statements. It appeared that for the hearing Durling was adopting the theme that he knew nothing and had never talked to anyone about the matter. In the inquiry he said that he had never talked to Salisbury about what happened to Maggie. He denied telling that the woman on the bridge that night was Mat Heath. He also denied "telling others" that his brother Palmer and Frank Crandall were the two men Dooley had seen on the bridge the night of the murder. Durling did admit to selling Salisbury the wrenches - the mysterious wrenches - but he maintained that it was four or five weeks before the "death of the girl."

Other witnesses, including Edward Barber, would later state that the Durlings were intoxicated most of the evening Maggie was murdered. They were seen asleep in a haystack that afternoon at 5:30. At 6:30 they were at Salisbury's, at 7:30 they were in Cowen's Hotel bar and at 8:30 they were at Frank Crandall's house. It would appear that they kept mobile, as their companionship was not sought by many that evening.

Besides the issue of his character and drinking habits, the very idea that Alfred Durling had not spoken to Horace Salisbury about Maggie's death is unbelievable. Middle Falls was a community of five hundred. If one person, a beautiful young woman, dies suspiciously it is impossible to believe that one of the town's heaviest drinkers would not speak of the death to his supplier.

When Horace Salisbury and his wife,
Emma, were called to the stand they contradicted Durling's earlier testimony. According to Salisbury, on or about October 20th, he had accepted from Alfred Durling a wrench as payment for part of his bar tab. Not sure of the origin of the wrench, Salisbury drove Durling to Justice Silvey's so that Durling could swear that he had sold Salisbury the wrench. On the way the two men had a very interesting conversation. Alfred told his driver that if his brother ever "let out on him," he would tell a tale that would have him (Parm) strung up. On the way home they passed the place where Maggie's body was found. Salisbury had remarked "if that log could talk, it would tell some wonderful things." Durling responded, "Yes, and if Mrs. Heath would talk she could tell some wonderful things." Durling also said that if the cause of Maggie's death came out it would be shown that Mrs. Heath was deeply connected. There was no explanation as to how Alfred Durling had come by this knowledge or if it was only speculation. What it did show was that Durling had spoken of Maggie's death to Salisbury.

Mrs. Emma Salisbury also discussed in the makeshift court the conversation she had with Alfred Durling. She had employed Alfred on occasion as a handyman. She said that Alfred told her that Parm had robbed a man between Middle Falls and Greenwich. Alfred said that if he needed he could tell things that "would go hard on Parm." Mrs. Salisbury told the court that Alfred had thought he had an acceptable relationship with   Mrs. Heath but that since Maggie's death the old woman had stopped waving and barely acknowledged his exis-tence. Alfred had told Mrs. Salisbury he had obtained the wrench from Mrs. Heath.

For whatever reasons, White did not recall Alfred to determine the source of the wrench or his relationship with Mrs. Heath.

Charles Salisbury, an aspiring jockey and the son of Horace and Emma, was called. He only made two contributions to the inquiry. On the morning Maggie's body was found he saw Mrs. Heath and Mrs. Teft talking outside Mrs. Teft's house. This conversation happened after Mrs. Teft told him of the drowning. Mrs. Teft would play a significant part in the case as she was with Dr. and Mrs. Scott the previous evening at the show. When Charlie went down to see the body he was the only person there. It was his recollection that there was a collar still on the dress.

The importance of the collar should not be missed. For some time there were reports that the collar on Maggie's dress was missing. The implication was that if the collar were ripped it would imply that Maggie had experienced some level of vio-lence. A suicide victim would not rip her collar before taking her life. It was believed that in her struggles the collar had been torn. There is also the possibility that if buttons had been bro-ken on the collar it would give further indication that a serious blow had been inflicted.

The next two witnesses,

Aaron Bristol and Chris Coleman, talked in substance about the collar. Coleman remembered the collar being on the body when he first saw his sister-in-law on the bank of the pond. Undertaker Bristol took the clothes from the dead girl's body. He did not remember there being a collar on the dress. He

108

could not explain how the collar could have gotten lost as the body was only handled by Deputy Skiff and Will Wilson.

Chris Coleman, in addition to Mrs. Teft, explained the sequence that people came to know of Maggie's death. Mrs. Teft was driving into Greenwich when a man told her of the drowning. She was not sure the identity of the man but she was certain it was not Reuben Stewart. A curious person, Mrs. Teft went down the embankment to look at the body. After she came back up she continued on her way to Greenwich. In Greenwich she saw Dr. Scott and told him of the discovery of Maggie's body.

The final witness of the day provided the foundation for an exciting conclusion. Lewis Potter, a farmer from Easton, had attended the show at the Opera House and was sitting next to a friend, Steve Lockwood. Potter remembered that at about 9:00 he had seen a man in a light overcoat and a slouch hat enter the theater and talk to an usher. The usher pointed in the direction of Dr. Scott, who was sitting near the front in a seat in the second row. The man then went up to Dr. Scott and whispered in his ear. The man and Dr. Scott both left the hall together. Potter, who was sitting in the gallery, could not hear what the two men said but he thought the incident peculiar enough to mention it to his friend Lockwood to whom he remarked "who the devil could that fellow be and what he does he want with the doctor."

Potter's remarks, which supported those of James Mulligan who testified in January to seeing a similar man, later the same night in the Scott's bar, proved too much for the doctor's composure.

The doctor asked

that if, before the witness was allowed to leave the stand, he could ask a few questions. The doctor closed with a plea to the attorney, "Mr. White there has been injustice shown to me in this case."

White's retort struck at the heart of his concern. He denied Dr. Scott's request with the answer, "It occurs to me, Dr. Scott, that you take more interest in this case than any other man in the county."

Dr. Scott immediately responded,

I think I should, I have a reputation at stake. There has been enough said that I was out that night. I can bring 5, 10, 20 witnesses who will testify that I did not leave the house that night. And furthermore, my wife, who was very feeble at that time, sat in the second seat from the last and would not go down near the front for fear people would notice her.

The choice of seats selected by his wife plays much differently later in the investigation.

With a long overdue arrogance toward the good doctor, James White closed the dialog with, "Dr. Scott, if you are indicted for being an accessory in this murder, you will have ample time to prove your innocence."

The hearing continued on Friday
with a series of witnesses selected to either support or contradict the testimony given the previous day. The day began with Mrs. Ecyclesymer and her daughter who went on the stand telling what had been reported earlier in the text. It was left to the interpretation of those in the room to determine if Scully did in fact have some special knowledge of what had occurred.

Rosa Alwell,
who was believed to be the last person to see Maggie alive, told

of seeing her with the empty pail. Miss Alwell had said "hello" and Maggie had returned the greeting. The real substance of Alwell's testimony was that she also saw Ed Boyd. It was Alwell's assessment that the two could have passed each other and had time to speak. Alwell was put on the stand to cast a shadow back on Ed Boyd who had been pretty much cleared as a suspect.

Dr. Scott's behavior again came into question when the last witness that morning, James Mulligan, took the stand. Mulligan had testified in January that on the night Maggie died some man in a light overcoat had come looking for Dr. Scott and that the doctor had left with the man. In the month between his first testimony and now, Sam Skiff, the deputy sheriff, had visited Mulligan. Skiff had been sent by Dr. Scott to try to get Mulligan to sign a statement that his January testimony was untrue. Mulligan refused to sign the statement. He went on to tell the court that days later while he was in the post office he overheard four men threaten to "roast me the next time they got me out." Mulligan did admit he was unsure if Dr. Scott's team was out that night.

Dr. Scott's character

came into question with the next two witnesses. Hiram Clark was one of the young men who worked at Dr. Scott's hotel. Since the murder, Clark had left his employment at Dr. Scott's hotel and was now working at the Hamilton House. When the show was over on the night in question, Hiram was sitting in the barroom. Dr. Scott told Hiram to go out and hitch up his team so Ed Barber could take them away. Hiram was not certain whether Dr. Scott went out with Barber or not.

Hiram's mother, Mary, was called to clarify a rumor that she was supposedly saying that Dr. Scott's team, which had

111

been rented was back in the stable by 6:00 p.m. On the stand she was asked to correct the time to 8:00 p.m. Because her son had been asked by Dr. Scott to tell her to change her testimony, she said it was her mistake and the correct time was 8:00 p.m. Obviously Dr. Scott was working overtime to cover all his bases. The time was very important to Dr. Scott, as he did not want there to be time for him to get the horses out again that night. Mary Clark was a very nervous witness exclaiming at one point, "I don't know anything about the case – you understand that?"

The day ended with Edward Scully being held while trying to raise his two hundred dollars bond. They wanted to be sure he would be present for a grand jury scheduled for the next month in Salem.

Although the report of the testimony of the witnesses that appeared in The *People's Journal* was close to the same as that of the other newspapers, the editorial in the same edition was very different than their competitors. This is of course with the exception of *The Whitehall Chronicle*. On the point of the scream heard by St. Mary as he drove his team into Greenwich the evening of the murder, the editor wrote "the scream which was heard on the road near the Heath house was not connected in any way with any other occurrence, which will aid in the investigation." The editor never said what evidence he used to dismiss the testimony. He did summarize the feeling of many when he pointed out "nothing of great value has been discovered by the inquiry", however he did not speak for everyone when he said "the investigation has been thorough and that everything possible has been done to learn whether it was foul play which caused Maggie's death."

Again the hearing was adjourned

this time with no specified date when it would reconvene. The community's frustration was becoming overwhelming. At this point, after what had been days of inquiry and months of finger pointing, there developed a minority feeling that the persons involved may not have come from Greenwich, Middle Falls or Easton.

Between the February hearings and those in March there were two letters of denial published in the local newspapers. These letters were written by people whose names had been raised in the February testimony. After reading the testimonies of the Salisburys and Kate Lansing, Mrs. Heath wrote a letter in which she denied any involvement with Maggie or the incidents that happened that October evening. In mid-March Will Wilson wrote a letter to justify all his actions, which were beginning to be considered incriminating. Wilson had been prodded into this public letter by an anonymous letter published in *The Post* that questioned his motives.

Mrs. Heath's letter

was dated February 9th and was written as a rebuttal to the testimonies of Mrs. Lansing, and Horace and Emma Salisbury. Mrs. Heath spent the first paragraph explaining that she was vilified and felt indignant to the point that, "it is the earnest duty of those so maliciously slandered to speak and denounce them [their accusers] publicly."

In the second paragraph she denied knowing or talking to Maggie. She claimed that she only went to the pond to accompany her farm tenant to see who was drowned. She didn't even recognize Maggie until someone said that it was "Herbert Reynolds's servant girl." She also denied knowing Reynolds or Alfred Durling.

again began to become the driving force behind the case.

On February 14th *The Post* fired a covert volley when it published a letter signed "An Interested Investigator." The "Investigator" exonerated Boyd and Herbert Reynolds by citing times given by the various witnesses. In the investigator's theory Boyd never saw Maggie but rather he passed the Reynolds house while Maggie was inside. The more serious part of the letter was the insinuations made about liveryman Wilson who kept conveniently reappearing. The involvement of Wilson was covered in a letter of rebuttal he wrote which was carried in full later.

The editor of *The Whitehall Chronicle* fired the opening direct volley with an editorial that said, in short, that because no person was accused, the death must have been a suicide. The editorial was well written but misconstrued the evidence. This editorial was a classic example of bending and twisting information to prove a preconceived opinion. After referring to Scully's detention as "the mouse that this mountain has brought forth," *The Chronicle* expressed its opinion clearly. "It seems the blood and thunder theory of Maggie Horrigan's death is utterly exploded." In the editor of *The Chronicle's* opinion there was no murder to investigate.

On March 6th, *The Peoples Journal* republished *The Chronicle's* editorial without adding any comment, effectively endorsing the opinion of the editor. By using *The Chronicle's* editorial *The Journal* was able to put forward an opinion without the potential backlash that generating their own theory would have created. This may be considered a cowardly act but *The Journal* needed to be mindful *The Post* was always looking at them as a target.

On March 7th *The Post* carried an editorial that picked apart the evidence that *The Chronicle* had used in its editorial the previous month. These editorials kept the case in the public's mind, printed peoples' questions and synthesized the conflicting theories that were being debated. In fairness these editorials served a second purpose, as the editors needed to sell newspapers. At this time these editorials were the closest thing people had to the televised debates carried today on the cable networks.

The "Interested Investigator" letter

of February 14th played heavily on the connection between Dr. Scott and Wilson. It also challenged how convenient it was that one or both of these individuals seemed to be at every crucial juncture of the case. To many, the "Interested Investigator" was really Editor Smart using a pseudonym to generate his opinion.

Another individual wrote several questions to both the publishers of *the Post* and *The Journal*, using the pen name "A Farmer." These questions, which were always thoughtful, often preceded the editorials in *The Post*. If Smart was this "farmer" he chose his second pen name well. Many of his readers in this rural county would have been farmers and they would have wanted to see themselves projected as the wise person asking relevant questions.

For reasons never articulated, March 6th, a month after the hearing had closed, was the day *The Journal* selected to speak out with its ideas on the case. On that one day, the newspaper carried two significant articles relating to the Horrigan murder. The first was Wilson's letter in response to the letter from the "Interested Investigator." The second was the editorial from *The Chronicle*.

The letter written by Wilson, or more likely by Wilson

in conjunction with Dr. Scott, addressed most of the relevant points in the "Interested Investigator's" letter. It was up to the reader to determine if the responses were true and how much weight should be placed on the explanation given.

The letter attributed to Wilson

is carried below exactly as it appeared including emphasis, grammatical and spelling errors!

> "I will be hanged if some external viltian,
> Some busy and insinuating rogue;
> Some cogging, consuming slave to get some office;
> Have not devised this slander, I'll be hanged else!"
> Shakespeare, Othello, Act 4, Scene 2.

Ed. Journal, - Some weeks since, a writer whose name, but not identity was hidden under the *nom de plume* of "Interested Investigator," favored the readers of the "*Post*" with innuendoes and aspersions regarding myself, the fine "Roman hand" of this sneaking assassin is visible all over your contemporary, and therefore his actual name is known to all intelligent readers. It is a misnomer and does not fit him; but let that pass. In simply mention the fact to let him see that his sneaking behind a pen name does not hide him from reprobation. My object now is to categorically deny the suggestions and statements of this "busy and insinusting rogue" giving him the "the lie direct," he says,

"Whether Scott's team was in that vicinity that night is open to speculation; whether it was or not, does not seem to appease the public in their apprehensions. Livery man Wilson, who does his business near Scott's hotel and of whom Scott hires when he hires at all, has for some time been engaged in advertising that he can account for Scott's whereabouts throughout that night."

This is lie No. 1. I have not been busy "*advertising* that he (I) can account for Scott's whereabouts," at the same time as there is no secret at all about Dr. Scott's whereabouts on the night in question. I fail to see where this "*Smart* Aleck's" point comes in.

Let us go a little further:

"This is the same Mr. Wilson that conveniently turned up at the brook as soon as the girl was found and kindly volunteered, I am told, to help take her out. He then drove to Mr. Coleman's, the brother-in-law of the girl and feelingly tenders his services by way of driving him down to identify the girl, saying to him that somebody thought that he would know her: while in the meantime and previously, Scott had presented himself at Coleman's and broke the sad news to the family."

Here are several lies by inference. I was *accidentally* not "conveniently", returning from Schuylerville, having taken a party thither in the course of my ordinary business, and I was *directed* by Mr. Skiff to go to Coleman's and inform him. It had already been decided that the girl was a relative of his. Any man with ordinary humanity would "feelingly", as he puts it, break such sad news. What about it?

Again I quote:

"The next we hear of Mr. Wilson he is engaged as assistant to Scott and Murray in doing the autopsy. A queer selection indeed. Who, before this, ever heard of a young man like Wilson being engaged to assist in the autopsy of a young girl, and frequent inquiry has been made as to who was responsible for it."

In reply to this, here is my explanation. I have always been employed by the undertakers, Jones & Bristol, in their business, and in the sad but sacred office of preparing the dead for burial. I, of course, did not assist in the autopsy proper, though I made myself useful in other ways. Here the "cogging, cozening" slanderer lies again, and whatever there was of indecency in my decent and orderly participation in these last sad offices is bred by his own revolting mind. There is *no significance* in youth or set in the presence of death, and I am disgusted that anyone even an anonymous slanderer, should suggest it.

Let me nail another lie to the wall, as one would vermin:

"Wilson consulted a spiritualistic medium in behalf of himself and Scott to ascertain whether they were guilty and the medium informed him that she knew of none more so than he."

This is an unqualifiedly false. I never consulted a medium as to my guilt or the guilt of Dr. Scott. On the face of it this assertion of drivelling idiocy; a so-called medium did assert that it was a case of suicide, but how this connects with my "guilt" I cannot see.

Again it is said:

"The person, with the light overcoat, that went into the Opera house that night for Scott tallies well with that of Wilson."

I must stab my pen through this as another lie. I certainly wear a light overcoat now, but it was bought nearly three months *after* the time referred to, I then wore a dark one.

Once more I quote:

"At the last hearing, I was credibly informed, that when the officer reached Greenwich, Wilson was one of the first to join him, following him to the justice's office and remaining there until Scully was taken out upon the street, and continued with him in his travels, where strange to say (and very unfortunate perhaps) Scully was "fetched up" at Scott's Hotel, where he remained until far into the evening. All this may mean nothing or it may mean a great deal."

Of course the fact here perverted – not stated – means absolutely *nothing*. I had been all the previous day driving the detective from place to place in search of Scully; what more natural than that he should desire to speak with me. Besides he had a reason. He desired me to walk with him for the reason that if we were seen conversing, others justifiably inquisitive would be to an extent prevented from accosting him and asking information. By his request I went to the Justice's office and waited and walked down with him. As for the boy and his staying at Scott's I suppose detective Price knows his own business best, and I certainly did no seek control of it on this occasion.

The fact is the "Post" man has an axe to grind, and he has done it to his own satisfaction, but he is a cowardly liar, none the less. I have broken silence not because I feard that any one would give credence to his slimy, venomous vaporings – especially those who know me – but because it is not well to let a lie go uncontradicted at any time.

The quotation from the great poet with which I head my letter, applies not only to the midnight sneak over whom I have wasted my time, but to another, who in the name of justice is making "confusion worse confounded" in this sad case.

I am sir, yours truly,
W. S. Wilson

There is one point in Wilson's letter that requires further examination. In the last paragraph he indicated that the quote that he opened with was meant for two individuals, the editor of *The Post* and "another." It obviously is not the Pinkerton detective, as he implied Price and he were nearly friends. That left only District Attorney Hull or James White, the Greenwich attorney heading the examination. One has to wonder why not both. It would appear that Wilson, if not everyone in Greenwich, felt that White, not Hull, was by this point truly leading the inquiry.

On March 7th *The Post* trumped *The Journal* with a thoughtful examination of the evidence and an attack on Dr. Scott. *The Post* wrote off the woman on the bridge Boyd saw the first night, as not being Maggie. *The Post* did not identify the woman but rather said based on the testimony of Remington and Mrs. Herbert, who put Maggie behind Boyd in Middle Falls, as it would have been impossible for her to get to the bridge ahead of Boyd.

It is *The Post's* attack on Dr. Scott that is more key. *The Post* pointed out that after Maggie's cousin, James Mulligan, testified that he saw a man in a light coat approach Dr. Scott that Dr. Scott sent Deputy Skiff to get a statement that the evidence given was not true. When it came out that the Clark boy was telling others that the doctor's team was back at the hotel by 6:00, Dr. Scott made him correct himself and his mother who was believed to be saying the same. To the editor of *The Post* it was a small step to believe that Dr. Scott, or one of his agents, had gotten to young Scully and made him change his story also.

On March 26th

the second inquiry reconvened for the third and final session. On this occasion it was obvious that the real purpose was to deal with the rumors generated during the January and February sessions of the investigation and pursued in between in the battle of the newspapers.

The first question addressed

the quality of the investigation done by Detective Price. William Harrington, a policeman from Greenwich, had accompanied Price when he went in to interview   Mrs. Heath. When they got to Mrs. Heath's house, Harrington disembarked from the carriage and went to the house to speak to the woman. While Harrington was on the porch, Price drove off and left him. Mrs. Heath refused to talk to Harrington until she had woken her son John to serve as a witness. When John finally got to the porch Mrs. Heath and Harrington talked for about ten minutes. The entire conversation was about how Price had left Harrington.

Harrington attributed Price's behavior to his being drunk at the time. According to Harrington he, too, had had a couple of glasses of beer but was sober, unlike his fellow officer.

Wilson was finally put under oath to clarify his involvement in the case. Wilson maintained that he owned eleven horses but none of them were out the night Maggie was killed. Wilson also said the Dr. Scott was not at his barn that night but that he had seen Dr. Scott at the play where the doctor had been sitting in one of the front seats. Wilson could not provide and alibi for after the show since he went home at 11:30 and directly to bed.

As he had done in his letter to *The Journal*, Wilson explained that he was an undertaker's assistant; therefore, there

120

was no significance to his being in the room while the autopsy was taking place.

Edward Scully

was recalled and contributed nothing beyond what he had said in February. When asked why he lied about the story about Maggie, Scully said it was partially for fun and the rest to pass the time. White recommended that Scully be released from custody on the condition he stay at home and behave. The boy agreed to the conditional release then told a reporter that he was heading west as soon as he could raise the money. Scully assured the reporter that with his special knowledge acquiring the money would not be a problem.

Henry Cipperly,

the man who provided a boy with a ride the morning Maggie's body was found, told the court that it was Scully but that they had not discussed anything relating to Maggie.

There were only two other witnesses

that day that added anything significant to the inquiry. On the night Maggie was picked up, Mrs. Catherine Remington was jostled by a well-dressed stranger in a light coat and black derby between the Reynolds house and the post office. This would have been minutes before the time Maggie was abducted. Unfortunately for the prosecution Catherine was sure that she would not be able to identify the man if she were to see him again.

Mrs. Peter Martin lived about four hundred yards from where Maggie's body was found. Her home was on the road that was perpendicular to the road to Greenwich. That evening her children had laughed at something they heard come from a wagon that passed the house then stopped in the vicinity. The wagon stopped on the road for about a half and hour. Under White's strict questioning Mrs. Martin's memory "became cloudy."

Peter Martin

was the first witness the next day. By this day, five full months had passed and the entire area was desperate for some finding. Martin testified to the same facts as his wife. The difference was that the day after Maggie's body was found Martin had walked up to the place where the wagon he and his wife had heard had stopped. He found that the horses had been hitched and the occupants of the wagon "went up" into a grove.

Mrs. Eliza Smith

did nothing to resolve the questions that had been raised. She lived in one of the few houses between the Reynolds home and the post office. On October 18th Mrs. Smith was home watching out the door. She testified to facts that contradicted every other witness. She said that she saw Maggie get the milk very early in the evening. She said she did not see Boyd for a full fifteen minutes after Maggie had passed. Mrs. Smith also placed Mrs. Kate Lansing at her house at 6:45 - ten minutes before Kate testified that she left her own house. Mrs. Smith also said she saw another woman with Rosa Alwell, who had testified she was alone. Mrs. Smith's testimony indicated that she had superior night vision. While everyone else was struggling to see ten feet Mrs. Smith was able to swear to the identity of people thirty or more feet away on this very dark night. Whatever her true motivation or memory, Mrs. Smith had enjoyed her fifteen minutes of fame.

Kate Lansing

testified for the third time. Her only contribution in addition to the other testimony she had provided was that she claimed to see the collar on Maggie's body before they took her body from the water. She also admitted that she was acquainted with Mrs. Anna Teft, which by this point implied that her testimony might be tainted.

Dr. Scott's wife,

Mary, was called to the stand to substantiate her husband's alibi for the evening. She told Justice Mansfield that she had attended the show with her friends Mrs. Anna Teft and James Wells. The three of them were near the front row. According to Mary, after Dr. Scott was finished selling tickets he took a seat across the aisle from her. She was able to see him for the rest of the performance and she assured the justice he never left the theater. Mrs. Scott confirmed her husband's testimony that she was not feeling well that evening. She was so indisposed that she was accompanied back to her hotel by Mr. Wells. She did not see her husband again until he came to bed at 2:00 a.m. Mary believed that her husband was in the barroom during the intervening period. She went on to say she knew that the team had gone out in the morning and had not returned until the evening. When asked how she knew about the team she said the manager of the hotel had told her so.

As White was about to release Mrs. Scott her husband rose and suggested he ask why she believed her husband was in the bar from after the show until he went to bed.

Attorney White accepted the doctor's request and asked the question. Her answer was classic and left the doctor open to even more speculation, "the doctor is a rather loud talking man and has a very peculiar laugh. Our sleeping apartment is directly over his office. Being sickly at the time I did not go to sleep until after he had come to bed. I could hear him below for the reasons given." The doctor most assuredly smiled as his well-coached student had performed as directed.

The doctor had in fact lost the exchange. His wife was supposed to say how she knew he was in the barroom not in his office. What she had actually stated was that he was not where he claimed to be. More important, when in January a witness had said that the doctor was approached in the theater by a man in a light coat, the doctor had stood up and told the court his wife was sick and she would not sit in the front for fear someone would see her. On the stand she had said just the opposite.

There was one point on which White would agree with the good Mrs. Scott – the doctor was a loud speaking man.

The other element that was suddenly becoming apparent was the degree to which Mrs. Anna Teft was involved. Anna was the person who accompanied Mary Scott to the show. She was also one of the first people to see Maggie in the pond. She had told Dr. Scott and Wilson of the drowning. Anna was also one of the people who initially said she saw Maggie walking toward Greenwich. She later said it was probably someone else. Anna was also the person who told Mrs. Heath of the body in the pond.

By now witnesses

were doing anything to forget facts and disassociate themselves from the proceedings. This was evident when Samuel McGrouty was called to the stand. Sam was only definite on two things. He was sure of his address and that he did not go to the show.

George Foster

was the last witness to contribute to the investigation. Foster was at the pond while Maggie's body was still in the water. Although he did not remember any collar he did remember blood around her fingernails. As Foster remembered it, Mrs. Anna Teft did not recognize Maggie while her body was in the water. Foster had immediately concluded that Maggie had been put in the water after she was dead. Given time and the information from the numerous witnesses he had not changed his mind.

James White and Justice Mansfield

were discussing whether to adjourn the hearing without a further date when Edward Scully, the father of fourteen year-old Edward Scully who had been arrested, stood and began talking to the crowd gathered. White called Edward to the stand and he told a tale that brought the family back into the center of the case. According to Edward on or about November 7th, when his wife was washing the dinner dishes, she looked out the window and saw a man's face looking back at her. Hearing her scream, Edward leaped to his feet and went to the window. Through the glass Edward asked the stranger what he wanted. The man told Edward that he needed to talk to him. Edward told the interloper that he couldn't open the door so the man needed to go to the front door. Fearing the man had a compatriot waiting in the dark, Edward waited till the man was on the porch before he opened the door. When the light of the opening door hit the man, he stepped back suddenly and put his hands in the pockets of his coat. The man on the porch was tall and heavy. He was wearing a light-colored overcoat with a slouch hat. The description exactly matched the one previously given of the man who had approached Dr. Scott in the theater.

In the light Edward could see the man's face clearly. Edward asked the man what he wanted and the man said he wanted Edward to come out in back of the house to talk business. When Edward asked what kind of business the man said "very important business." After hearing the man ask him to come out back, Edward was even more afraid the man had a confederate waiting, so he insisted on knowing the nature of the man's business. In an effort to draw Edward out, the man finally admitted the business in question was the Horrigan case. At this point Edward became even more apprehensive, believing the man thought he knew something of the case and wanted to "rid the world" of him.

Edward asked the man where he lived and the man answered Greenwich. Edward said, "That is funny, I have lived here for the last three or four years and have never seen you before." The man then changed his story and said he lived in Middle Falls. Edward said I have walked to Middle Falls every day for the last two years and "I never seen you there."

Edward then asked the man his name and the man gave him his real name. The man seemed nervous and kept putting his hand in his coat pocket as if to draw a weapon. The man kept insisting that Edward go out back with him to discuss this "murder scrape." Edward refused, insisting that he had worked that night and knew nothing of the affair. Exasperated, the man turned and walked toward the back of the house, the same direction in which he had arrived.

Edward's daughter watched the man through the window and at one point thought he was going to turn around and return, but after hesitating for a moment the man went on.

Some time later Edward Scully noticed the man at an auction being held at the Hamilton House. He asked several people the man's name and learned that the man was Lawton Wilbur of Easton. This is the same name the man had used when he called at Scully's house.

In checking with his family Edward learned that this was not the first time he had been seen around the Scully house. About a week before or roughly the first of November the same man had come by when he was out. Edward's daughter opened the door and told the man her father was not home. The day before the man had come to the porch his son had gone to the store to buy a newspaper. When the boy returned, he saw the same man hiding behind a hedge studying the back of the Scully home. The man first ducked down to avoid detection but as the boy went into the house he saw the man jump the fence and leave the area.

The natural question was, why had Edward Scully waited so long to come forward? In his own defense Edward named three men who he had told the story to at the time that the incidents occurred.

A warrant was issued for Lawton Wilbur and Deputy Sheriff Teft was sent in search of the new and only suspect. The hearing was adjourned until 2:30 to provide time for Deputy Teft to pick up Wilbur.

At 4:00 Teft returned with the news that Wilbur could

not be found. Not wanting to waste the entire afternoon, White called Charles Reynolds, a blacksmith assistant in Middle Falls. Charles's only contribution was that, like so many others, he had been to the pond where he helped carry Maggie's body to the wagon. He remembered the collar being on the dress.

On Friday the hearing was held for the final day. White had Edward Scully repeat his testimony from the previous day. The reporters were impressed by how earnest he was when he spoke. Overnight they were able to locate Wilbur. When he was placed on the stand he denied all of Edward's comments and said that he could prove where he was the night that he was supposedly at Edward Scully's house. He was not asked to provide proof or where he was the night Scully had said he came to his house.

There were three final witnesses. Capt. D. A. Sisson who had been a sailor and barge captain all his life had also seen Maggie's body when it was taken from the water. He testified that he had seen over twenty drowning victims in his career and none looked like Maggie. They all had their eyes and mouths open. The other victims all had their legs drawn up toward their chests and blue faces. In contrasts Maggie's body had been flat as if laid out in final repose with her face a natural color.

Father Field, the priest at St. Joseph's Church in Greenwich, was called to discuss whether a Catholic would consider suicide. Father Field said that all Catholics feared not being permitted to be buried in hollow ground, so they would not consider suicide. He said that in a person as holy as Maggie this feeling would be so strong it would "carry with her even in a fit of insanity."

The last witness was Edward Scully's other son, Thomas, who supported his father's testimony about a man hiding behind the hedge. The one major difference was that the boy was nervous and unable to identify Wilbur.

Feeling that they had stabbed at every possible suspect,

White and Mansfield agreed to adjourn the hearing without setting a date to reconvene.

The second set of hearings had occupied seven days over a two-and-a-half-month period and resulted in the temporary arrest of a fourteen year-old boy and a lot of finger pointing. Most of the people in the hamlet of Middle Falls had been called. Nothing was certain except that members of the Reynolds family were probably not involved.

Despite the re-occurring testimony, where people said that they had not formed an opinion as to what had happened, everyone had an opinion but there seemed no way to prove any of them.

Unanswered questions

continued to fester in the community even after the hearing had ended. There were major questions and minor ones both outstanding. Some of the major issues included:

- Was Maggie's death a murder or a suicide?
- If she was murdered who committed the act?
- What was the motive?
- Had Dr. Scott tried to aid Maggie while she was still alive?

There were also minor issues including:

- Where was the collar for Maggie's dress?
- Where did Durling get the wrench?
- Why would anyone have called on the senior Edward Scully in connection with Maggie's death?

The biggest problem is that without a suspect the case would not die.

The Inquest Never Returned

to public session after it was recessed in April of 1890. The investigation, like the courtroom inquiry, never formally ended but rather seemed to just slowly fizzle out. In any event, the only individual ever charged with any crime relating to the incident was young Edward Scully and he was released without even having a hearing.

For a variety of reasons it appears that not all of those embroiled in the mystery were publicly questioned. The circumstances seem to imply that the coroner's jury started to believe that those guilty had learned their lesson and the situation would not be repeated. It is almost as if the jury had come to the realization that one life had been destroyed (Maggie's) and since it was an "accidental murder," what would be gained by destroying the lives of those involved in the assault?

Regardless of the quality of the investigation there are several essential facts that can be made based on the hearings.

- Maggie Horrigan was murdered probably by accident. Despite arguments made by *The People's Journal* that Maggie committed suicide, the simple fact is that it would have been impossible for Maggie, or any other person, to have a head injury that rendered her unconscious and then somehow drown herself.

- More than one person was involved in Maggie's abduction and subsequent death. The fact that Maggie had gone quiet so quickly after her brief outcry which was followed almost immediately by the sound of the wagon, would imply that more than one individual was present. At the very least one to hold her and one to drive the wagon.

- To commit an act such as abduction with the intent to have sexual relations, the men involved would most likely have been very close friends and very likely under the influence of alcohol.

- The vehicle that the men who assaulted Maggie used was formal. The description of the carriage indicated it was designed similar to hacks of the period. Witnesses said the driver was outside on a raised seat while the passengers could be protected by a convertible type cover. This meant that the carriage was designed to have a driver exposed while the passengers sat comfortably in the rear. If an individual owned this type of carriage, he would be someone of substance, since he would be able to employ a driver. If, however, a livery owned the carriage, it would probably have been rented by someone who wanted rather badly to impress.

The district attorney had made a point

of calling most of the single Irish males and all the single men in the community who were not originally from Greenwich. The implication was simple - the perpetrator of this crime could not be one of the boys from the upstanding families of Greenwich. This tactic ultimately backfired. Those that Hull and White tried to blame were able to publicly establish their alibis, while those not brought to the stand were never granted the scrutiny of an examination. The choice, not to put the sons of the local families on the witness stand, set up a situation where the whereabouts of most of those from the community were never officially established.

Over time and through rumors many of the young single males and even some of those that were married were incriminated by their neighbors. To this day there are names still thrown out among the people of Greenwich. Through a hidden code of trust, those from the outside are never brought into the discussion. The names are only shared with family, close friends or associates. Researchers are left to follow a few subtle clues as to whose names were smeared. Why people over one hundred years later try so hard to cover the identity of those suggested in the rumors is a mystery. It only takes one trip to one of the many copies of the census to determine who were the males not included in the examination. A second trip to the vital records is all that it takes to establish connections. Yet to this day, many of the citizens of the village of Greenwich continue to try to mask a secret that in all probability was never theirs to conceal.

In the case of Maggie's murder there was a group of three sixteen-year-old boys from Greenwich who were logically – in the social class struggle of the times - to have their names associated with the crime. These three were either related to members of the coroner's jury or their fathers were politically connected. The involvement of these boys is possible, but not likely. There are two reasons these names are bantered about. The first is their fathers' power and influence. Greenwich, despite its tranquil appearance, is like most communities, where it is not as important that your child succeeds as it is that your prosperous neighbor's child fails. If the son of a successful person goes astray, the event is almost a cathartic for those who have had little success in their lives. For this reason, the failures of the children of the rich are always looked upon with exhilaration. The second reason these boys' names were bantered about is their knowledge of the area. The probability that they would have known about Maggie, the pretty Irish lass is great. Based on the records they would have seen her walking to church on Sundays. This knowledge of Maggie and their knowledge of the community would have been important, since it is probable that the perpetrators knew of the barn near where the body was found. There is also the very real possibility that these boys had a wild side, but that is impossible to determine at this time.

The reasons for excluding the local boys are simple. First, some of the people in the audience of the theater that night would have recognized any local boys if they were the ones that approached Dr. Scott. The man who went into the opera house in the light overcoat had to be someone from out of the village. Second, their fathers, as powerful as they may have been, would not have been able to silence the entire community. As we will see, Dr. Scott elected to leave town almost immediately, yet these boys all stayed for years.

The pattern

of a community taking on a self-imposed silence regarding a local mystery as it is today may have been the same in 1889. There is no doubt that the coroner's jury was selected from among the most connected men in the village. By their nature these men would have known everyone of substance. It was because of these connections and the comment by the boy Scully where he said that the persons he saw that night were from homes better known than any in the newspaper to that date that caused the rumors that the perpetrators were local to persist and expand. Young Scully's comment kept the question in the public's mind, were the perpetrators from wealthy families?

There are only two possible conclusions

to the behavior adopted by many in the community of Greenwich. Either these people were right and by their silence they were protecting a group from the village, or they were wrong and the persons who attacked Maggie were from out of the hamlet.

The problem of not facing the issues relating to Maggie's death is exemplified by the position held by *The Peoples Journal*. This one newspaper maintained that Maggie's death was a suicide long after all the other newspapers, except one, were calling it a murder. The purpose of *The Journal's* position is still unclear. Did the editor believe that if you tell the people that it was suicide often enough they would come to accept it as fact? This idea should be questioned as the editor actually participated in the offer of a reward for information leading to an arrest and conviction of Maggie's assailants. Was the editor trying to cover for someone? If so, who? It would be logical to assume that the editor would cover for a friend or a friend's son. Yet a cover-up is not likely, as there were very few young local men out and about that night. Was the editor covering for someone out of town? Perhaps the cover-up was for someone of great political influence?

The story would not end in 1895

despite the efforts of *The Peoples Journal*. The editor of *The Washington County Post* had held the story in the community's mind for five months during the winter of 1889-90. The numerous and speculative rumors within the county kept Maggie's unsolved murder in the minds of the public for years to come. Eventually her story was replaced by events more compelling to the people at the time.

The Carriage that was used to abduct Maggie

Maggie's Revenge

began with a series of mysterious deaths, five years after the hearings ended.

The story of Maggie Horrigan

had the potential to slip silently into obscurity. It is true that for one generation rumors persisted and everyone in the area had an opinion but, like all unsolved crimes where the victim left little family to seek revenge, this one had the real promise of evaporating from the records. There is, however, a very real reason to believe that her humble Irish voice would not acquiesce without justice being served.

Note: the *events* listed from this point forward are all true. The question is whether or not they are related to the death of Maggie. The answer to that question is left to the reader; however, the text is written as if there is a connection between the various occurrences and Maggie's misfortune.

In the spring of 1895 there were a series of newsworthy circumstances that could best be construed as revenge for what had befallen Maggie. The ultimate retaliations started the first week in April of 1895 with the death of a businessman from Fort Edward, Dim Hinckley.

From the moment that young Scully first told his story, a second set of rumors as to the perpetrators had started. These rumors implied that those responsible for Maggie's murder were from the village of Fort Edward not Greenwich. One of those named in rumor was forty-five year-old Dimick (also spelled Dymick and Dimmock) Hinckley.

By 1895, Hinckley had been a partner for ten years in the lumberyard of Teft, Hinckley and Company in Fort Edward. Prior to joining in the partnership, Hinckley had learned the business from his father, a lumberman in Glens Falls. Between his jobs in Glens Falls and Fort Edward, Hinckley had also had a position in the lumberyards at Thompson Mills, which are on the Hudson River between Fort Edward and Middle Falls.

To those in Fort Edward

who accepted the rumor that the perpetrators were from their community believed Hinckley was the driver of the carriage that picked up Maggie that fateful October night back in 1889. There was some basis for the rumor as it had been established that Hinckley and Al Woodin hired a carriage from Well's Livery in Fort Edward on the night of the murder.

If it were the case that Hinckley was involved, to provide as much of an alibi as possible he would have had to drive the team the seventeen miles back to Fort Edward as fast as the horses could travel. The team would have been breathing heavily when they arrived back at the livery. During the intervening years it was accepted by the people that the best description of the rented team was they were exceedingly lathered when they were returned that night.

There is another reason that implies that Hinckley served as the driver. There are two logical ways from Fort Edward to Greenwich. One goes through the low rolling hills into Argyle. The second is to follow the Hudson River south and cut up into Middle Falls. Hinckley, having worked in Thompson Mill, would have been most familiar with the latter route and therefore have taken it on a black night to get to Greenwich.

At 8:30 in the morning on April 2, 1895,

Dim Hinckley died of consumption (TB) in the village of Hudson Falls. In the first articles concerning his death, Hinckley was described as an industrious man of "strict integrity." Forty-five year-old Hinckley had left a widow, Harriet, a grown son, Frank, who lived in Saint Louis, and two daughters, Maude, a bookkeeper, and Anna, who still lived at home.

Probably because his death was both protracted and anticipated, coupled with the gossip of his having been the driver, it was inevitable that a rumor of a deathbed confession of a prosperous businessman would erupt. This story, however, began immediately and simultaneously in Hudson Falls, Fort Edward, Argyle and Greenwich. The "news" was that before he died Hinckley confessed to his minister of his involvement in the abduction and the subsequent death of Maggie. In the tale the names of other well-known citizens were included.

Before one takes a position on the truthfulness of the deathbed confession, one needs to understand a conviction held by many at the time. It was believed that if a person confessed on his deathbed to violating any of the Ten Commandments he would be forgiven and through confession would be accepted into heaven. For those trying to live as they chose yet ultimately receive God's blessing, this last minute plea offered an attractive option. Hinckley may have been enticed by his associates not to ask for forgiveness until the very end, allowing them time to explore their options.

To its credit *The Sandy Hill Herald* went to the home of the minister of the Methodist church to try to determine if there was any truth to the gossip. According the account that ran in *The Herald,* and most of the other regional newspapers, the Reverend Yates was happy to give an interview in an effort to thwart the talk.

The Herald said of the good Reverend:

He was mortified to think that his name should be connected with such a malicious story that has no foundation whatever, and cannot fail to wound the feelings of several worthy families to gratify the petty spite of small minds, who feel aggrieved at some supposed injury.

To try to set the record straight, Yates wrote a quick note, which he preferred be published as written in the newspapers. Yates recognized in his note that he had "attended a citizen...who recently died." In the message he went on to say, "The rumor that this man made a confession of a great crime acknowledging his guilt, are entirely and absolutely false. They have no foundation whatever, I regret exceedingly that such cruel reports should be set afloat by evil minded persons, that have a tendency to bring sorrow to many worthy people."

It is important to note that Reverend Yates did not officiate at Hinckley's funeral. Reverend Forte of the Baptist church led the final service. Mr. Forte was quoted as saying from the pulpit that Mr. Hinckley had not confessed to murder. Forte left open the possibility that there may have been a confession for accessory to murder.

One would have thought that the letter from the minister would be adequate to clarify the record. For reasons that will never be totally understood, Edgar Hull, the district attorney and the man who had led the official investigation into Maggie's death, decided to add his voice to the efforts to stop the rumors. He said in a letter to the regional newspapers that he could not sit idly by and watch whole communities proclaim an innocent man involved in Maggie's abduction. What was not in the letter was that the man in question was a friend of Hull and Hull's son Frank. The only logical explanation for Hull's letter was that the very appearance of Hinckley's entanglement in an unsolved murder might imply that as district attorney, he had not done all that was required in investigating the circumstances in Maggie's death. Hull aspirated to run for the Supreme Court. He needed to have as clean a record as possible.

Hull's decision to write the letter is conjures up that infamous phrase from Shakespeare's Hamlet. "The lady doth protest too much, me thinks."

On April 12, 1895,

Hull's letter appeared in *The Peoples Journal* and *The Press and Review* which was published in Salem. Both newspapers carried the same letter written by former District Attorney Edgar Hull. In both the Greenwich and Salem newspapers, the letter was addressed to the community. It should be noted that *The Washington County Post*, the newspaper that had always felt that the investigation was incomplete, did not provide space for the letter.

Hull used this letter as an opportunity to explain his view of the Horrigan investigation and the circumstances of Hinckley's death. Hull's letter is so relevant that it is printed in full - emphasis is added to parts that will be discussed later.

Fort Edward, April 5, - Maggie Horrigan was found dead in a pool of water at Greenwich, on the morning of October 19, 1889. *The last time she was seen alive was when she was walking from Middle Falls toward the village of Greenwich, between seven and half past seven o'clock, on the evening of the 18th of October.*

She was buried as a suicide. I ordered her disinterment and a second autopsy was held, which discovered a wound on the back of her head which rendered her unconscious or dead before she was placed in the water.

Over two hundred witnesses were interviewed and a large

number sworn before the various investigating tribunals.

Two of the best men of Pinkerton's detective agency, the best officers of Saratoga, Rennsselaer and Washington counties investigated the case for months.

Trained and experienced reporters, who I regard as better than detectives in such cases, made the case one of close study and thorough investigation.

One branch of the investigation which is material to the purposes of this statement, was the investigation of livery stables located in Greenwich and surrounding towns, in order to determine who had let livery rigs that night, and then to follow up and trace the rigs and the persons who hired them.

One of the livery stables then investigated was that of George Wells, of Fort Edward.

The investigation showed that Albert Woodin and Dimick Hinckley hired a team of Wells that night. They drove out of the livery a little after seven o'clock. At about the same time Maggie Horrigan was walking from Middle Falls towards Greenwich, a distance of about seventeen miles from Fort Edward. Hinckley and Woodin, with this team, were at Glens Falls at about nine o'clock that evening *in the company of two other persons whose names I will not state,* drinking wine at a Glens Falls hotel. Between 10:30 and eleven o'clock they returned the team to Wells's livery stable. *These facts were proven before a grand jury at Sandy Hill as shown by the stenographer's minutes.*

Hinckley died of consumption last Tuesday morning. Within two hours after his death a story had started simultaneously in Glens Falls, Sandy Hill, Fort Edward, Greenwich and Argyle, that Hinckley had made a confession to his spiritual advisors, Rev. Yates and Rev. Forte that he had killed Maggie Horrigan. The story was pronounced false in the newspapers by a note elsewhere by Rev. Mr. Yates, and from the pulpit by Rev.

Mr. Forte. So far as the living are concerned they can answer for themselves. *But I thought as I lowered Hinckley's coffin into his grave that I would answer the lie by using the records of the grand jury.*

According to Hull's letter

"The investigation showed that Albert Woodin and Dimick Hinckley hired a team of Wells that night. They drove out of the livery a little after seven o'clock." The Wells mentioned by Hull was George Wells who operated a livery in Fort Edward (Wells's name will appear again later). Somehow it was established that Dimick Hinckley and Allen Woodin had taken out one of Wells's carriages that evening. Hull determined, to his own satisfaction, that Hinckley acquired the carriage at 7:00 p.m. Conveniently, that was at the same time Maggie was being abducted in Middle Falls. It was, therefore, impossible, in Hull's mind, for Hinckley to have been involved in a murder seventeen miles away from the stable. Other receipts from this same stable note the date of a sale or rental but make no reference to the time that the rental started. It is unlikely that the evidence used in the investigation was anything except testimony, as it is implausible that there existed an invoice that had the time the carriage was leased. What is far more significant is that Wells owned a carriage similar to the one described by the witnesses.

In the former district attorney's statement was a reference to Albert (Allen) Woodin. Woodin would be an important name that would play heavily into Maggie's revenge three months later. Through his letter, Hull admitted to those in the region that Woodin had rented the carriage with Hinckley. Why had Hull thrown Woodin's name into the story? Was it that he assumed that by adding Woodin's name it would somehow reduce the theory that Hinckley was involved?

Setting a time of approximately 9:30 p.m., Hull went on to say that Hinckley and Woodin were seen *"in the company of two other persons whose names I will not state."* This group was in a tavern in Glens Falls on the evening of Maggie's death. Hull finished his assertion by saying that the carriage was returned to Wells's Livery at 11:00 p.m. If Hull accepted the story that Hinckley and Woodin had rented the livery at 7:00 p.m., it would have made it impossible for them to be in Greenwich at the time of Maggie's murder. It is interesting that given the carriage was let at the same time as the abduction the investigation continued to look at the alibi of being at the hotel in Glens Falls. Given this much detail in the alibi was provided, why then does Hull not state the other two names? Woodin's name had not been associated with the confession, so why was it so prominently added by Hull? Why had he bothered to pursue where Woodin and Hinckley went later that night or when they returned the carriage?

There was another interesting note in Hull's letter of defense. Not only were Hinckley and Woodin at the hotel in Glens Falls but they were also seen in the company of two others - bringing the number to four - the same number of persons as in the rumor.

There is one even more engaging sentence in the letter. The second sentence reads, *"The last time she was seen alive was when she was walking from Middle Falls toward the village of Greenwich, between seven and half past seven o'clock, on the evening of the 18th of October."* That Maggie walked alone toward Greenwich was never proven and was almost certainly not true. Why then in a letter meant to vindicate a suspect would the man who headed the investigation have put in such a profound untruth? Could it be that he believed a story told by only one witness even though that witness later retracted the story? Could it be that he wanted to believe that that was what happened because what really happened was just too personal to be accepted?

Perhaps the extent and depth of Hull's misrepresentation is best evidenced in the line *"She was buried as a suicide."* Maggie was not buried as a suicide. Father Field was satisfied that she was murdered. On the day after her death her funeral service was held in a Catholic church and she was buried in sacred ground.

Hull wove facts and impressions well creating the fabric of a story that could, if allowed to stand on its own, be mistaken for truth. Rather than naming who saw Woodin and Hinckley he told the readers that, *"These facts were proven before a grand jury at Sandy Hill as shown by the stenographer's minutes."* Hull had to know it would be very unlikely that anyone would bother to check such a record. It is important to understand that the grand jury would only determine if there existed sufficient evidence to warrant a trial. It is not now, nor was it then, the role of a grand jury to find someone guilty or innocent. It is very probable that by citing the grand jury's record Hull was trying to imply Hinckley had been found innocent at a higher level than just his decision as the chief law enforcement official in the county.

Why would the district attorney go to such lengths to refute a rumor? Perhaps it was his proximity to the target of the rumor. After all, Hull was so close to Hinckley that as, *"I lowered Hinckley's coffin into his grave that I would answer the lie by using the records of the grand jury."* District Attorney Edgar

Hull was actually a pallbearer!

As much as many would have liked the issue to stop at this point, it refused. In point of fact this was only the beginning of the tragedies.

TOOK HIS OWN LIFE

was the headline in the newspaper on April 25, 1895. Only three weeks had passed since the death of Dim Hinckley. The previous evening at about 6:30 the young son of Frank Morgan went into the family barn and found his father suspended from one of the rafters by a rope around his neck. The reports in the newspaper were that Morgan had been ill and despondent of late. Morgan was the next-door neighbor of Hinckley.

County Coroner Pattee called a jury to determine the cause of Morgan's death. Pattee was a physician in Fort Edward and coincidentally Morgan's brother-in-law. Under Pattee's guidance, the coroner's inquest questioned several witnesses. In their findings they recorded the time period of Morgan's depression as two to three weeks. This was exactly the amount of time that had passed since Dim Hinckley's death.

Morgan was a blacksmith by trade, but a politician by desire. He had served his fellow citizens of Fort Edward as a village trustee. In 1893 Morgan had run for the state Assembly seat for his district. More important than his background was Morgan's home. Morgan lived directly across Canal Street from Dim Hinckley. Morgan and Hinckley were the same age. They were also members of the same volunteer fire department. In simplest terms, they were close friends.

The Reverend Forte of the Baptist church also served as the official at Morgan's funeral service.

Then on June 9, 1895,

John Weston, an employee of the pulp mill in Fort Edward, took an early morning stroll along the east shore of the Hudson River. He needed to take this walk as he used the small piece of land near the river to graze his cow, which he was on his way to milk. When Weston looked over the high bank near the end of Seminary Street, he saw a male corpse floating in an eddy in the river. Knowing there was no current to wash the body away, Weston immediately went for help.

At this point in the river there was only a narrow path on which to climb down the steep bank to the small shore. Despite the impediments of a cramped trail and sheer bank, in a matter of minutes the lifeless body was pulled from the water. Like vultures that gather at the site of an animal corpse, many of Fort Edward's citizens rushed to the scene upon hearing the news.

Based on the science of the times, it was understood by everyone at the scene that a body had to be in the water for at least four days prior to its discovery. As with Maggie, the idea was that a drowned victim stayed underwater for a period of at least three days, then the corpse would float to the surface.

Since everyone in the community knew the victim, the body was immediately identified as that of, Page, one of the members of the volunteer fire department. The entire community knew that Page had been missing for several days and search parties had been out looking for him. A quick visual examination showed that there were no marks on the body that would indicate that Page had encountered violence prior to his death. There was no evidence of a robbery as the deceased was still wearing his watch and diamond ring. Exposure to the water had caused the watch to stop at eight o'clock. A quick examination of his clothing indicated that personal papers were found in the jacket.

It had been only two and a half months since Morgan's

death, and Dr. Pattee was again summoning a coroner's jury, as required by law. Despite ample evidence to the contrary, the reports in the newspapers all made the death out to be an accident, not a suicide. One witness was called to testify that Page had been stumbling more recently. The implication was that he had fallen into the river and had not deliberately entered the water.

At the time of his death, Page was suffering from what the newspapers said was a long-term mental disorder officially classified as insanity. Page seemed fearful that someone was out to injure his father, daughter and himself. Dr. Hun of Albany had diagnosed Page with "general paresis." Dr. Hun noted the symptoms in a letter to Page's parents. Part of the letter said that the disease would be demonstrated by:

> a slow but steady failure of mental powers, and it is not usually necessary to confine the patient in an asylum. The course of the disease, however, is sometimes interrupted by outbreaks of a good deal of violence and especially toward the end of the disease. In such cases of course it is necessary that the patient should be removed to an asylum, but in other phases of the disease the patient can just as well, or even better, remain at home, and I should certainly advice you to keep your son at home at the present time. I have no hope whatever of his ultimate recovery.

Early in his life Page had been a strong swimmer but one of the symptoms of his condition had caused a partial paralysis of his right arm. Page's disability was all the more painful to his parents who had seen their promising son become a lawyer, marry well and now his wife and law practice were both gone. Perhaps the family's sadness was even greater since Page was the son of District Attorney Edgar Hull.

Over the previous two years Page had become literally attached to his only daughter, Nellie. For Nellie he would spend any money he could raise and over whom he "kept vigilant watch." Raising money was an issue since as a result of what was projected as being his condition, Page was no longer able to practice law.

Although prior to his death Page had not been violent, he had been intimidating. Page, it appears, was also consumed with protecting his father from presumed enemies. One named "enemy" was Page's own uncle, whom he was certain had attempted to injure his father with a screwdriver. If any person came to visit his father during the evening, Page would appear in the doorway then move to stand behind the guest. When the guest left, Page would follow him or her to the edge of the property. It can be safely assumed that this behavior tended to keep the number of visitors to a minimum. Any time his father left home Page offered to walk with him as protection. During the day as people entered his father's law office Page would go to the door and stare at them. At night he would wait for his father to go to bed then sneak down to the bedroom door and listen silently to be sure his father was safe. The most serious action was when he gave his father two Italian stilettos to be locked up. Page was fearful someone could get the knives and kill someone.

In startling contrast,

if someone came to visit him, Page, whose given name was Frank, acted dramatically different. Upon hearing of the guest Page would either take refuge in his room, where he would lock the door and pull down the curtains, or he would run out the back door of the house and stand on the river bank until the

147

guest had left.

Despite his problems,

Frank "Page" Hull's actions for the past several months indicated to his neighbors that he was not inclined toward suicide but rather he was bent on protecting himself and those he loved. The neighbors cited as evidence that he was not bent on suicide such events as he was planning to travel to Lake George with his parents and daughter. They also noted that on his way to the river he had stopped to borrow a hat. It should be noted that the above statements were taken from published newspaper accounts.

Frank Hull had begun his interest in a legal career as a young man. He worked for five years as a page in the state Assembly. As a result of his early career, throughout his life Hull was known, as "Page", not Frank. Young Hull was admitted to the bar as soon after he came of age as possible. Although only thirty-three at the time of his death, Hull's obituary notes that he had been considered one of the most promising lawyers in the region. The county's judges considered him a natural lawyer based on the clarity of his written and verbal arguments. Five years before, it was evident that his career as a lawyer was only beginning and he was considered to have a brilliant future. Page Hull had served as justice of the peace for Fort Edward for two years and secretary of the State Firemen's Association.

The week preceding the discovery of Page Hull's body was not pleasant for him or his family. During the period of Monday night through early Tuesday morning was the first time that Page exhibited indications of violence. On Monday evening he had retired early. In the middle of he night his mother heard him speaking loudly. He was calling out for someone to care for his daughter, Nellie. His mother arose and, like all loving parents, went to care for her ailing son. His actions were so strong that his mother was fearful that the disease had taken a turn for the worse. Mrs. Hull eventually persuaded her son to get dressed.

Dressed, however, has a different meaning in this situation. First Page put eleven pairs of socks in an earthen jar and poured water into the jar. He then put on his shoes without any socks. During this entire episode Page kept telling his mother that is father was going to kill him and that she should take care of Nellie. From all the reports Page suddenly was seeing his father in a very different perspective then that reported earlier. Prior to this, Page was his father's protector now suddenly he saw himself as his father's victim.

Mrs. Hull walked with her son to the living room where he sat with her on the lounge. Eventually Page quieted down and after kissing his mother's cheek he fell asleep on her shoulder. The peace ended about 4 o'clock that morning when Page again started to call out that he had heard his father tell a man that he had a reason to kill his own son. He resisted his mother's embraces and kept trying to jump out the window to flee. With the grace and peace only a devoted parent can show in this type of situation, Mrs. Hull was able to get Page settled one more time. Eventually she was even able to get him to eat some breakfast. While at the table, suddenly, and without any warning, he stood up and started for the river. By this time his sister had gotten out of bed. She, being dressed and the younger of the two women who were with Page that morning, followed him for a while. Page escaped her pursuit by jumping over a ditch and continuing north.

Page made several stops on his trek toward the site of

the old Fort Edward Institute. He first stopped at Doty's store. He picked up a hat, telling Doty not to mention it to his father, as the former district attorney was going to kill him. While going up Mechanic Street, Page told the story that his father was out to kill him to three other people - Bartholomew Ford, Mr. Keech and a Mr. Groesbeck. When Page got to the Sheehan house he stopped and talked for five minutes, again repeating the same story with a slight twist - that his father was going to shut him up.

Page then went across the pasture in back of the old institute and was last seen at 6:40 walking up the railroad tracks in the direction of Glens Falls. Fearing for his safety, a group of volunteers soon began to follow the route Page had taken. When they got to the first flag man north of the pastures they were told that Page had not passed.

There was confusion as to where Page went after he was last seen walking up the tracks. A handkerchief was found in the woods near the track. To his family the handkerchief was proof that he had taken refuge in the thicket. Many others, who were less hopeful of a fortunate outcome, felt that he had gone to the river. For several days the people of Fort Edward took what time they could spare and looked for the son of one of their most prominent citizens. Hundreds of people participated in the search. Until the discovery of his body, Page's parents were sure he was hiding in the woods in a state of exhaustion.

Frank Hull may have had two traits which were listed as assets in his obituary that, in reality, were more likely his undoing. This assumption is based on the theory that Page was in some way involved in Maggie Horrigan's death. Hull was considered a "determined fighter" who would "never acknowledge defeat." The second fault noted as an asset was his loyalty to his friends.

Edgar Hull and John Woodin, the father of Albert Woodin who had rented the carriage with Hinckley, were founding members of the Satterlee Hose Company on Broadway in Fort Edward. Page had followed his father as a member of the same fire company. Page had been president of the company and the secretary for the State Firemen's Association. Coroner Pattee, Frank Hull, Edgar Hull and John Woodin were all friends and all were members of the fire company, as were Dim Hinckley and Frank Morgan.

According to the obituary in the Glens Falls newspaper, the members of the Satterlee Hose Company attended Page's funeral en masse.

If one assumes that Page was involved in Maggie's death, did his father the district attorney know? Was Page afraid his father would find out and that is why he kept such a vigilant watch over his father? Did fear of exposure lead to paranoia? In the end, did Page realize his father had learned of his involvement, so his fear shifted from exposure to his father to certainty that his father wanted him punished?

In the coroner's inquest, documents give us a very different picture than the one gleaned from the newspapers. The coroner's report stated that Page had only been suffering from the mental issues for two weeks. The newspapers implied the problem had been longer in duration.

Allen Woodin,

Page Hull's best friend since childhood, was struck by a train less than three weeks after the death of Page. Allen D. Woodin was the son of John Woodin, a deceased associate of Edgar Hull's. Allen was struck and instantly killed by the northbound sleeper train at the place that is now the overpass in Fort

Edward. The accident happened about one o'clock in the morning.

There are two different stories concerning the circumstances of young Woodin's death. In the newspaper obituary, Allen was said to have been sitting on the porch of the Waverly House. He then decided to cross the tracks to the Eldridge House when a freight train from the north approached. While he was standing on the tracks looking at the southbound freight train, a passenger train coming from the south struck him. According to the obituary he was thrown against a telegraph pole and his head was crushed. Woodin was killed immediately. Coroner Pattee, the same man as was called for Morgan and Page's deaths, was called to lead the investigation.

The obituary pointed out that for the last few months before his death, Allen Woodin was in the livery business with George Wells. This is the same Wells that had rented the livery to Hinckley and Woodin the night of Maggie's death.

The second report of the train accident is directly attributed to the research of William H. Hill, a local historian who had become fascinated by the Horrigan story. In one of Hill's scrapbooks, found in the Hill Collection at Adirondack Community College, are handwritten notes surrounding Woodin's obituary. In his notes Hill pointed out that Woodin was supposedly involved in Maggie's death. Hill had interviewed Charles Thebo, who was sitting with Woodin on the porch of the Waverly House the night of the accident. Hill's notes about the interview with Thebo read, "and as the train approached he arose, recited a verse of poetry and deliberately stepped in front of the sleeper."

Let's examine these circumstances
as if Maggie was somehow able to reach out and avenge her

own death with the most fitting of punishments.

Could it be that the rumors were true and Hinckley was the driver of the carriage? In the necessity of escaping the scene, and in an effort to get back to Fort Edward as early as possible, had he driven the horses till they were out of wind? If that scenario were true then would Maggie's spirit have wanted Hinckley to die from the slow strangulation of consumption?

Remember, according to Abraham Cipperly, Maggie had called out something to the effect of "don't do it!" Could Allen Woodin, in an act of desperation to have her be quiet, have hit Maggie on the head, crushing her skull? Then in her retaliation, Maggie had him hit in the head by a fast moving train?

To these two chronicles we add the mysterious drowning of Page Hull. Whoever placed Maggie's body in the water did so with a strong understanding of how to avoid detection by making the death look like a suicide. The foremost persons at knowing what evidence would be examined are the police and lawyers. Could Page have been the person who suggested that they place her young body face down in the brook to simulate a suicide? In revenge, would Maggie's spirit have him drown in his beloved river?

But Maggie's death was attributed to asphyxiation, not drowning. In fact no water was found in her lungs. Could Frank Morgan have alleviated Maggie's suffering by strangling her? Then, in retaliation she had him hang himself?

The events

listed in this section of *Maggie's Revenge* are all true. The question is, what are the connections of these events to the murder of Maggie? Skeptics should read this unsigned letter, which appears in the Hill collection, before disregarding the possibility that the four men's deaths were to avenge Maggie's.

There is a small handwritten note attached to the letter that needs to be included. This note provides us with a history of the letter. It also indicates that Hill attempted exhaustive research in this case. Mr. Hill had several notes handwritten on the letter. Most of these notes appear at the bottom.

Mr. Hill,

The attached is from the mother of my friend in Chicago. I thought it might interest you.

    K. Hubbard

She typed this mess. (message) and then had a nightmare.

       I was just a little girl when it happened. Maggie Horrigan was much older than I, but I knew her well, as she use to come down to Pearce's next to us in Scheidam. He was her uncle. Maggie was tall and nice looking, real pretty. I was with her the week before she died. She was at her uncle's and she and I went over to watch the evening train come in. I can remember how pretty she looked.

       The night it happened, Maggie was going to visit some friends. She worked for some people in Middle Falls. I don't know how old she was, but I think I was about twelve.

       The night it happened two men (names withheld) were on their way back to Hudson Falls or Glens Falls. They were both lawyers. They must have scared her to death. It happened by the stone bridge in Middle Falls, and they must have jumped out of their horse and buggy and grabbed her. They found her coat and hat on the bridge in the morning, but there was frost under them when they found them. They say that the night it happened there was a play at the Opera House, and some one sent in for Dr. Scott and Billy Wilson and they think that someone called them to Middle Falls to try and revive her. I guess when they saw how bad she was, they brought her into old Mrs. So and So's house to try and do something. This Mrs. So and So's house didn't have too good a name. So, the next morning someone saw her coat and hat on the bridge and when they investigated, they saw her body down by the brook with her face in the water. When she was laid out in the Undertakers, she was in the coffin right in the window, all you had to do was step up to the window to see her. You could see the cut on one of her fingers, as though it was made from some one's finger nail. The Journal was full for weeks. The two lawyers both committed suicide.

The following are the margin notes made by Hill:
- Scheidam was the name the locals used for the south end of Middle Falls.
- Hill points out that after they took the body to Mrs. So and So's they moved it to Sherman's barn.
- Mrs. So and So was Mrs. Mat Heath. Hill felt that this letter was his first direct link between Heath and the crime.

There is a major problem
with this entire logic that needs to be addressed. The murder was most probably an "accident." An accident in the context that the men did not seek to murder Maggie, but they were most probably intent on rape. In his research, Hill never made a connection between the four men. This may have been because he knew of them and worked from the assumption that anyone would understand they were friends.

Even the rape theory was troubling, since most rapes that make the news are done by individuals not groups. The few group rapes or molestations reported have a certain fraternity mentality. Therefore, there needed to be some connection between the men that would indicate that they had a bond so strong that they would commit an act as vile as rape together.

Frank "Page" Hull and Al Woodin had grown up together in Fort Edward. They were born the same year and as young men lived just houses away from each other on South

Broadway, Fort Edward. Their fathers were close friends and members of the same fire company. At the time of the assault or shortly after they were both separated from their wives. They were both living in the Eldridge House on Broadway in Fort Edward in October 1889. They had both moved out of Fort Edward in 1892 but had returned by 1895. Additionally they were both members of the same fire department, the same one their fathers started. Although no one of these factors proves that the two men were close, when taken in combination, the bond is evident. Add to the relationship the fact that Page, as the educated lawyer, would most certainly have been the intellectual leader of any group.

Morgan and Hinckley were similarly connected. They were approximately the same age. The two men were neighbors who were involved in some of the same organizations. Hinckley had also separated from his wife by 1892. He was living with her again at the time of his death.

The link between the two pairs of men is the recognition by Edgar Hull that Hinckley and Woodin had rented the coach together.

Why Maggie?

is the missing link in this story. If only we could establish a reason why Maggie was selected. It would be compelling if the pieces of this quilt could be sewn into a fabric stronger than a locked safety deposit box.

Historian Hill did his best to develop a case. His theory was based on the assumption that whoever committed the act did so inadvertently. Hill believed the men were on their way to the play in Greenwich. As they passed through Middle Falls they saw Maggie when she went to get the milk. Attracted by her beauty, the men waited for to come back out of the

Reynolds house. When she came out to join her friends, the men realized she was alone. They grabbed her in front of the house and the rest was an accident.

This explanation may be correct but sets us on two courses that are rather far reaching. First, was Maggie that beautiful that men would, on a mere glance on a very dark night, sit and wait for her? Second, how did they know she would come back out? Even more of a reach is, how would they know she would be alone?

Hill missed many of the links but in his defense he was also the one that found some of the probable perpetrators.

The story would not end

for the people of Greenwich. A little over fifty years ago, *The People's Journal* ran a series entitled "Hearsay and History," to remind their readers of Greenwich's rich history. In May 1949 as one part of the series there was an article relating the story of Maggie's death and, to a minor extent, the investigation that followed. The article was a brief summary of the sequence of events, relating to Maggie's murder with perceptions of how the people at that time felt about the incident. The paper, sixty years after the occurrence, still tried to remain neutral regarding whether Maggie's death was suicide or murder. This is an interesting position since based on the evidence admitted into the court there is little doubt that Maggie was murdered. The only realistic question is whether the act was deliberate or accidental.

What was more important than the 1949 article itself were two letters of response written by readers. The first letter came from the former Susan Brown who was living in Shelbyville, Indiana. Susan's father was the man that held Wilson's team up on the road, while Wilson went down to the pond and pulled Maggie's body out of the water. This letter finally explained how the frost came to be under Maggie's hat and cape. The problem the frost had presented to the investigation was that it was accepted that the frost did not set in until early in the morning the day after Maggie was killed. For the frost to be under the shawl and hat the clothes would have had to have been placed on the log after the frost set in; therefore, many believed that those who were responsible for Maggie's death would have had to spend the night near the pond.

As a child, Susan, her three sisters, and her parents were living in the house on the Sherman farm near the site of stone bridge. According to Susan her sister was out early that morning and found the hat and shawl on the log.   Like any child with, what to them is a momentous discovery, her sister picked up the clothes and brought them home. When her father, Joseph Brown, found out about her removing the clothes he insisted that she take them back to where she found them. Probably like all children in a situation where they had to return something they were not supposed to have taken, she just placed them on the log, assuming the exact position was less important than the log as a location. The young child inevitably placed the clothes on a section of log where the frost had not yet melted. The cold clothes would have trapped the cold and held the frost.

With Susan's letter, we can finally understand how those who committed the act may have left early the night before and yet there was still frost under the clothes the next day.

Susan's letter went on to recount her memory of Maggie's body floating in the water. She told how she was present when the men took the body from the water and placed it on the sheets. Although it had been sixty years, the memory of an event of that dramatic importance was still locked in her brain. The effect of the murder of an innocent young woman on the village was best demonstrated by Susan's description of the community's reaction: "For months afterwards people came to the site and took chips out of the log where the hat and jacket were found." These could only be considered souvenirs of the macabre.

For the Brown family, removing the body from the water did not remove Maggie's presence. Mrs. Brown became afraid to live in the house and insisted that the family move into Greenwich. Was Susan's mother's fear based on a belief that the same fate might await herself or her daughters? Or was it based on a feeling that merely taking Maggie's body away did not remove her spirit from the scene? So insistent was Mrs. Brown that the family relocated within a year to a home in the village of Greenwich.

The second letter published in *The Journal* in 1949 was by local historian Sheldon Gill. Gill, for whom the local history room at the Greenwich Library is named, gives credence to *The Journal* article. His letter also added some color to the facts as reported in the article. Gill first admitted that the general public believed that a cover up was in place. He went on to say that the common assumption was that four young men of good families in Washington County were involved. Gill concluded by asserting that the community's judgement was that Maggie was "accidentally killed."

The following explanation of the men and their relationship to Maggie is directly from Mr. Gill's account in the newspaper. It should be noted that Gill never cited a source for his information.

It was their (the men from out of town) intention to attend the theatre and dance which was to follow the show. The boys were out for a good time and may have had a drink or two. On passing through Middle Falls they met Maggie as she was crossing the road for a pail of milk from a neighbor.

How these men molested Maggie is not clear. Probably she was forcibly lifted into the wagon. She screamed, and in an effort to stifle the screams she was smothered. Panic stricken they drove the team to the McMullen farm and under the shed, or into the barn there. The barn at that time was close to the road, just opposite the house.

Before examining the young men's actions that followed it should be noted that the McMullen Farm was the name in 1949 not in 1889. In 1889 this was the Sherman Farm from Susan Brown's letter. Gill continues by spending some time explaining how two of the men then went to Greenwich, seeking the aid of Dr. Scott with whom "they were acquainted." Gill maintains that it was understood that Dr. Scott returned with the two young men. Gill went on to tell of Dr. Scott's examination.

The doctor told them she was dead, and the body was disposed of in the manner which you have already been told. It evidently was their intention to make the death appear a suicide.

The story told by the boy, after he left Greenwich that he slept in this barn where the team of horses was taken, and that he overheard the conversation there was probably true. It fits into this account of what happened. When the boy was brought back to Greenwich, and placed under oath he recanted. He may have been a frightened boy, or possibly was intimidated.

Gill then explained why based on the depth of the water the suicide theory was false. Gill's examination of the depth of the water showed how he mixes the present with the past. He said the water was only six inches deep. Yes, by 1949 the millpond had filled in and was very shallow but at the time of Maggie's death it may well have been much deeper. An even bigger error was when Gill failed to mention the head injury, which was more significant than the depth of the water.

There are two more paragraphs in Gill's letter worthy of quoting. These paragraphs were not in sequence-in-between was information about Maggie's family and how the story broke slowly.

These four men all died a violent death, and a great many people believe they committed suicide. However, there was no evidence to support this opinion. The last one to die was struck by a train and before his death he is supposed to have made a confession of the crime. I only remember the name of one of these young men, and on making inquiry of some of the older people I find they also remember only the one name...

It must be remembered that these young men were not rough-necks, but respectable young fellows. It also must be remembered that, at great risk to themselves, they did seek medical help for the girl.

The words used above to describe the men were those of Mr. Gill not the author. My feelings are significantly different than Gill's. More consequential is how close Gill was to the names of the rest of the men involved. Building on what Gill already knew finding those who attacked Maggie would have been very easy.

The Hubbell Stables

Picture of ad for Hubbell & Wells

163

The Eldridge House

The Waverly

Music hall ensemble

TENORS AND BASSES.

Mr. Frederick Barkley,
Mr. Clayton Smith,
Mr. A. H. Wicks,
Mr. Melvin Mory,
Mr. Elmer Burnham,
Mr. David Taylor,
Mr. Frank Harris,
Mr. Philo Ingalsbe,
Mr. Martin Marshall,
Mr. Charles Thebo,
Mr. John Frank,
Mr. Edgar Durkee,
Mr. J. Earl Cheesman,
Mr. John J. Morgan,
Mr. A. M. Reeves,
Mr. L. E. Montgomery,
Mr. John Koch,
Mr. Wm. Niles,
Mr. Frank Hull,
Mr. Bert Vorce,
Mr. Myron Rozelle,
Mr. Geo. Osborn,
Mr. F. Osborn,
Mr. A. E. Plue.

So What Did Happen?

It is far more likely that Maggie was pre-selected, than she was picked up by random. In all probability the persons who abducted her either knew her or knew of her and were in Middle Falls on that evening with the intent of grabbing the young attractive Irish maid. It was in search of proof of this presumption that many trips were made to Fort Edward and Greenwich. There are some events and connections that are known that would lead us to a stronger bond between the assailants, a motive and Maggie.

Dim Hinckley worked for some time on the Hudson River in Thompson's Mill. In getting to Thompson's Mill from Fort Edward he would have been used to taking the River Road south. On a dark moonless night he would have preferred that route to Greenwich than by going through Argyle. If Hinckley were the driver he would have taken the river route which would have put him on the road through Middle Falls.

Within the two weeks preceding Maggie's abduction Page Hull had been elected secretary of the New York State Firemen's Association. This was only one year after he had been elected president of the Satterlee Fire Company of Fort Edward. His rise could only be described as meteoric, since he was not even an officer in the Satterlee Company two years before. Young Hull had a reason to be out celebrating, his political career was starting. From this base, statewide office was just a few years away.

In the same issue of *The People's Journal* that announced Maggie's death there was a mention in the social column that Allen Woodin's father, John, had been in Greenwich. Had he brought Allen with him? Is this the link? More likely the link was Frank Morgan. Morgan was originally from Lockport. The husband of Mrs. Mary McMaster, one of the guests at the Reynolds house that evening, was also from Lockport. It is most probable that Morgan knew Mrs. McMaster. If he did know her he may and probably did know of Maggie. It would have been easy to inquire of a friend the identity of this lovely maid. Her simple habits could have been learned, although most people went to get the mail every evening. It would be logical to assume that Maggie was among those who met at the post office.

What happened

to Maggie will never be known. There was nothing special in her routine the day of her murder. The difference was in the day of the men who apprehended her. It is the author's belief that Hinckley, Morgan, Woodin and Page Hull rented a carriage from Wells earlier than reported in Edgar Hull's letter. The four men left Fort Edward for Greenwich and a night on the town. They were probably celebrating Page's election. On their way they were drinking and bragging. One of them told the story of the pretty servant. The others joined in the frivolity and soon they decided either as a joke or in all seriousness to grab the young maid.

When they got to Middle Falls they saw Maggie as she went to get the milk. They pulled their carriage into the circular driveway between the church and Maggie's house. They most assuredly agreed that if she came out alone they would grab her. If her friends came along first they would just pull out and go to the play. Hull, who wore the light-colored overcoat, went out near the street to stand guard. Hinckley waited with the team. Morgan and Woodin slithered across the small lawn and waited for Maggie in the shadows of the maple trees. The ever polite and respectful Maggie, not wanting to have her friends bother her employers by knocking on the door, went outside to await their company for their evening stroll.

By the time Maggie came out of the shed door Ed Boyd had already passed and was on his way to Greenwich. When Maggie came out events flew into an accelerated rate. One of the men grabbed Maggie by her upper arms. This man was in front of her. She tried to scream so the man behind her put his hands over her mouth to stifle the outcry. His grip was so strong it caused Maggie's teeth to cut into her lips. The man who was driving the carriage pulled the team around to the side of the house. The two who were holding Maggie lifted her struggling form into the carriage. The fourth man, in his hurry to join his friends at the outlet of the driveway, bumped into Mrs. Remington as she was walking to the post office. At the end of the drive the fourth man – the - guard jumped into the carriage and the men drove on the dark road toward Greenwich and away from the limited lights of Middle Falls.

Vainly, Maggie continued to struggle in an effort to protect her virtue. The men laid on top of her to suppress her movements. The men laying down in the carriage is why Boyd was unable to see anyone in the coach as it passed him. The carriage turned on to the last road before Greenwich.

Maggie refused to be quiet and was heard by the Martins. In an effort to quiet her, one of the men grabbed the wrench and hit her with it. When she was hit Maggie went immediately limp. Her assailants first felt a moment of relief. As she started to fall, the man with the wrench dropped it, reaching out to seize her falling body. It needs to be noted that it was common for wagons to breakdown so all carriages carried a toolbox with them.

Realizing that she would not regain consciousness, the

men wavered between leaving her unconscious body and going for help. In an act that demonstrated that they were resourceful, if not wise, they decided to go for help.

Hill believed they went to Mat Heath's for help. He held that the reputation of Heath's home was well enough known that the men felt comfortable going there for assistance. Hill felt Mat would have known who would render help without asking too many questions. Hill might have been correct but, if the four are the men who are suggested in this book, they would have known of Sherman's barn and Dr. Scott without the aid of Heath. Mrs. Heath, based on her reputation, would have been assumed to have been involved even if she had nothing to do with the events of that evening.

Understanding the nature of their predicament, the men sought shelter, assistance and a rendezvous point. If Hull were involved they would have known of Sherman's barn, as Job Sherman was a fellow lawyer. Everyone who had ever been to Greenwich had to know of the boisterous Dr. Scott. Being in politics, Hull and Morgan would certainly have known of the doctor who was not practicing. Having worked just over the hill in Thompson's Mill, Hinckley would have known of the barn and Dr. Scott.

Not knowing that a young vagrant was sleeping in the haymow, the four men took Maggie's limp body into Sherman's barn. Two men, probably Morgan and Woodin, carried Maggie into the barn while the other two took the carriage into Greenwich in search of Dr. Scott. Hull would have gone for Scott since, if the doctor were to respond to anyone, it would be someone with Hull's influence. Hinckley would have served as driver. While they awaited their confederates' return, Morgan and Woodin did not want to stay with the body. These two went out on the road where they were seen by several passing vehicles.

At the Greenwich Opera House, Page Hull approached Dr. Scott who was sitting in one of the front rows. After whispering in the doctor's ear, the two went to the lobby to talk. After hearing of the dilemma, Scott sent Hull back to again check on the girl.

When he was sure Maggie had not regained consciousness Hull went back to Greenwich for Scott. By this time the play was over and Scott was back in his hotel. There Hull beseeched him to come to Maggie's aid.

Scott, knowing how to use and accept favors, went to the barn to treat the maid. Although well over two hundred pounds Scott was not a man to put himself at great personal risk. He asked Will Wilson to drive him to the barn. Wilson would serve as his bodyguard.

With an arrogance for which he was famous, Scott went into the barn fully intent on treating Maggie. In his efforts to examine her, Scott released Maggie's hair to check her skull. The men would not even consider pinning her hair back on top of her head. Scott tried to revive the young lady but his efforts were all for naught. In exasperation he said the line attributed to him by young Scully, "I have done all I can. Do with her as you please I'll not tell." Scott never did tell the truth about that evening.

The men decided that Maggie would never recover. One, in an effort to ease her pain, held something over her mouth and nose to suffocate her. The men then took her body out the small window in the back of the barn and down to the millpond. Gently, they placed her limp form in the water in an attempt to make her death appear a suicide. One of the men took her hat and shawl up to the log to give a clear indication as to the fact that a body was below. They felt guilty and wanted her body discovered and buried.

The four men then hurriedly drove back to Fort Edward in an effort to be away from the scene as quickly as possible. They had connections that could provide them with an alibi in Glens Falls. They were more concerned that one of the neighbors of the livery would see them when they came in. Like all men with a wild side, they were more afraid of those who knew and disliked them than they were of strangers.

As the morning dragged on, Scott became anxious. He had Will Wilson begin driving around the area to see if there was news that the body had been discovered.

There is the question of one other person's possible involvement. Reuben Stewart was the president of the Board of Trustee's in Greenwich. This is relatively the equivalent of mayor today and a very political position. It is very convenient that he discovered Maggie's body. It is also convenient that he was late getting to the bridge that morning. It is possible that Scott told him of the body. They expected one of the men working on the road to check when he saw the clothes on the log. When none of the men went to check by 10:00 a.m. Stewart went himself. Stewart's involvement is left only as a logical possibility.

Knowing Maggie's body would be discovered the next morning, Dr. Scott had already determined to keep himself above reproach by being as involved in the investigation as possible. At first, Dr. Scott assumed that meant serving on the coroner's jury. From the post of juror he would be in a position to have a direct say in the verdict. When Coroner Millington ordered an autopsy Scott realized he should control what was discovered about Maggie's death. Scott must have been delighted when they appointed young Dr. Murray as his assistant in the autopsy. Scott would have known that he could control Murray. One can only imagine the feeling Dr. Scott had when he realized that all his orchestrations could be wiped out in the second autopsy. Was it not until after Hull ordered the second autopsy that Dr. Scott told the district attorney of Page's involvement? That would explain why Hull literally dropped out of the investigation.

It was at some point after Maggie's body was removed from the pond that the collar disappeared. It may have been either Will Wilson or Dr. Scott who noticed the rip and realized that the collar would indicate foul play. In any case, one of these two palmed the collar.

What is unclear is how soon people knew of the political connections of the assailants. There is no doubt that Coroner Millington's jury was political. Did Scott arrange this jury or was it Stewart or perhaps even Hull? Most likely it was Scott, as he would have the most to lose and would have known how to call in favors if necessary.

That leaves the issue of the Scully family, Edward junior and senior. Junior was in the barn that night and witnessed what happened below. He probably recognized Page Hull from his previous dealings with his father over the horse theft. In an effort to raise cash, young Scully contacted Page, demanding money for secrecy. Page Hull knew immediately that he had to silence the lad. Page went to Hinckley with his dilemma. Hinckley knew Lawton Wilbur from his work in Thompson's Mills. Just as reported in the court, Wilbur went to the elder Scully's to find out the location of his missing son.

It is doubtful that any of this can be proved over one hundred years after the fact. The logic, however, is compelling.

1866 Map of Fort Edward

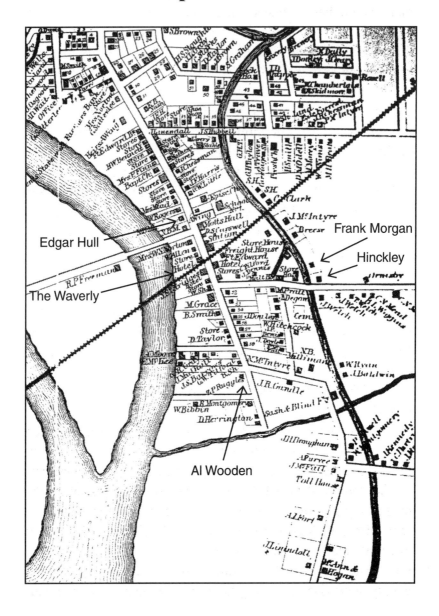

Edgar Hull

Frank Morgan

Hinckley

The Waverly

Al Wooden

174

In Defense of Edgar Hull,

there is no hard evidence that Page Hull was involved in Maggie's death. There is even less that his father knew for a fact of his son's probable entanglement. On the other hand, to serve as the district attorney for fifteen years, Edgar Hull would have to have been an astute perceiver of people's reactions, even his own son's. Edgar, like any father, may have wanted to believe his son was not implicated in any misdeed but his sense of the truth would have told him if Page were a collaborator. Even then would he have told his son he knew or tried to address the problem without a direct indictment? What other reason could there have been for the elder Hull to not be more actively involved in the investigation of the highly publicized local murder?

If Edgar did believe that his son was in some way involved in the abduction and subsequent death of Maggie Horrigan, readers will have to decide for themselves whether he took an active or passive role when examining the evidence. Before judging Hull too harshly people need to examine their own heart and what they would do for their own child, especially if they believed that the act was an accident and that the behavior would never be repeated.

We also need to examine Edgar Hull's character when trying to see if he would have covered for his son. In February of 1877, twelve years before Maggie's murder, Hull represented the people of Fort Edward as the town supervisor on the county legislature. As supervisor he became embroiled in a feud with the editor of *The Sandy Hill Herald* over the position of county clerk. The editor wanted to be appointed to the position. The editor of *The Herald* wrote a letter to each of the county supervisors, seeking their endorsement. Hull responded in writing that he had already promised his support to another candidate but that if the second candidate should withdraw he would support the editor. Not only did Hull renege on his word, he went further and condemned the editor, "hurling at us [the editor] the bitterest of invectives, and pouring out upon us [the editor] a torrent of personal abuse, as evidenced by his publication of private and confidential correspondence."

Hull should have known better than to get into a contest with people who buy their ink by the barrel and their paper by the ton. The editor retorted with an attack on the character of Hull. After saying how they had tried to maintain the highroad with respect to Hull the editor said that he did so:

with knowledge of the perfidy of his personal character. We might have applied the scalpel to his personal life and publicly dissected it, in the light of his past history and present career, revealing his associations with vicious men and bad women. We might have exposed his confidential relations with those who inhabit the debatable land between honesty and crime, and shown that all things sacred are held by him in supreme contempt. Might repeat the stories told of his indulgence in unlawful pleasures, at the expense of the reputation for chastity of the unfortunate female who perchance may come under his baneful influence.

The editor then pretended to return to the highroad saying how proud he was that he did not stoop to the level of Hull. The editor's reason was that this type of reporting was "…interesting to our readers." The editor did not end with this attack.

He went on to say:

> Impressed with the belief that the noxious dose of Hull was so strong that it would be rejected by the people of Fort Edward.

The editor closed his attack by saying that, although Hull was not his representative his influence was felt by all in the county therefore, Hull's political career needed to be stopped. He ended with a broadside about Hull the man.

> One whose private reputation makes decent men shudder, and whose public career can not be glossed over by any amount of fine writing is certainly not the man the town or the public need in the legislature of Washington county.

The readers can only ask themselves if the man described by the editor of the *Herald* could be the father of a man who would be a roughneck who would injure a girl for his own pleasure?

Epilog

For years after the deaths of so many members of what was to be the next generation of Fort Edward's leaders, Edgar Hull could be seen most evenings walking out onto the bridge behind his house. There he would have his after dinner cigar while looking at the water below.

What a mix of thoughts must have gone through his mind as he looked down on the moving water, the depth and speed of which was determined by the rain in the distant mountains. No matter how fast or slow the current each evening, not even the tenacious flow of the Hudson could erode the memories of the decisions made regarding the death of the beautiful Irish maid.

What Happened To...

Edgar Hull

died in August of 1929 just a little over two months before the infamous stock market crash. In many ways his life had crashed years before.

District Attorney Edgar Hull lived into his ninetieth year. He practiced law for sixty-five years. For fifty of those years he was the attorney for the D & H Railroad. He was also the attorney for the International Paper Company until 1923.

In 1890 there was a great political rebellion in Washington County. In that election, Edgar Hull was defeated in his attempt to continue to serve as district attorney. He was replaced by James White. In 1899, at the age of fifty-nine, Hull ran unsuccessfully as an independent candidate for county court judge.

Hull was very proud of the fact that the Hull family had played a significant role in the Revolutionary War and the War of 1812. He was so proud that his pedigree was noted in his *New York Times* obituary. With the death of his only son in 1895 the family named almost ended. Page did have one son, Edgar, who had moved out of the area. Page also had a daughter, Nellie, who was raised by Edgar senior.

Dr. Scott

moved to Troy in 1890, where he resumed the practice of medicine. In Troy he went into partnership with Dr. F. B. Smith. The two became specialists in the treatment of nervous and chronic diseases. He bought out Dr. Smith's interest in the Troy Magnetic Institute at 6 Union Place. Dr. Scott used magnets for the treatment of common ailments.

Dr. Scott died suddenly on July 17, 1917, at his home at 1821 Fifth Avenue in Troy. He was seventy-one at the time. He had a son, Walter, who became a physician in Niagara Falls. Walter was one of the young men in Greenwich who was of the age to be considered in the rumors revolving around Maggie's abduction. Lucky for Walter he was at Syracuse University the night Maggie was killed.

In Troy Dr. Scott was a member of the Methodist church and numerous Masonic Lodges. His wife, who was "weak" the night Maggie died, survived her husband.

Edward Scully's

parents, Edward and Mary Scully, had many problems with their children in 1890. In June of that year they lost twin boys, Charles and Joseph, one day apart. The boys were less than a week old. Edward, the boy in the barn, was released after the hearing in March 1890. His legal troubles did not end at that time. He was arrested again in August of 1890. This time the arrest was for theft from a business in Waterford. Although not yet fifteen, Scully had already been arrested five times.

James White

had spent his early adult life somewhat a wanderer. He grew up in extreme northern New York and was educated at Williams College in Massachusetts. In 1894, White became the district attorney for Washington County, succeeding Edgar Hull.

Editor Henry Clay Morhous

was the author of the *Reminiscences of the 123rd Regiment of the New York Volunteers*. The book was published in 1879. Morhous had been a sergeant in the Civil War and had maintained a diary of his daily life throughout the war. The book described the troop's movements and daily life in the camps. The history was published by Morhous's own newspaper *The People's Journal*. It is interesting to note that *The Journal* was able to double its size and totally revise its format in August of

1890. This enhancement was just five months after the investigation went into remission.

Throughout his life, Morhous was extremely proud of his service to the Union. He was active in the GAR, holding virtually all the major positions in the local organization. Morhous was also a member of the Greenwich Masonic organization, as had been Dr. Scott.

Morhous married twice. His first wife, Libby Knight of Whitehall, died the first year they were married. In 1872 at the age of thirty-one Morhous married a second time. This wife was Lillie Sickles of Valley Falls. Morhous died as the result of a heart attack at his residence in Greenwich on September 14, 1915. He was seventy-three at the time. He had outlived one of his two sons (William d. 1910), the other, Henry, took over the publication of the newspaper. Morhous was buried in Greenwich Cemetery.

The Durling Brothers

Al (45) and Palmer (32) both died within a week of each other the year after Maggie's inquiry ended. For those who may have believed that it was people on the lower end of the social ladder who caused Maggie's death would have been attributed it to the Durlings. If that was Maggie Horrigan's revenge, for the Durlings the wait was short. Alfred Durling died May 22, 1891, of pneumonia. Less than ten days later Alfred's brother Palmer died of heart failure. He had suffered for thirteen days.

Chris Coleman,

Maggie's brother-in-law bought the home of Mat Heath about a year after the murder and opened the house as a hotel. He died in 1895. By 1900, his widow, Maggie's sister Mary, moved into the house at 14 Church Street. Somehow the Coleman family had come into money.

Visiting The Scenes Today

will be like a trip back in time. The events reported in this book, took place in the hamlet of Middle Falls, or the villages of Greenwich, Cambridge and Fort Edward. These are all small communities within a reasonable radius to be covered in a day's outing.

Washington County is on the southern Vermont border and is, to a large an extent, an undiscovered place to holiday. The rolling hills, wood lands, open fields and engaging towns make it an interesting destination almost anytime; however the area is especially attractive in the fall and spring.

The scene of the murder

and the former homes of many of the people involved can be reached by taking either Route 29 east from Schuylerville, or Route 40 north from Troy. Route 29 can be reached easily from exit 14 of the Northway. After exiting the Northway follow the signs for Schuylerville. To get to Greenwich and all that is there, continue on Route 29 through Schuylerville. Just east of the Washington County Fair Grounds, state Routes 29 and 40 become one for about a mile. The hamlet of Middle Falls is on this short section of highway where the two routes are merged. The hamlet begins just after you cross the bridge over the Batten Kill and continues to where Route 40 turns left. The scenes in the map of Middle Falls are on this stretch of road.

The Reynolds house

where Maggie worked is the first large two-story brick house on the left, after the bridge. This home has recently been remodeled. Luckily, the house still has the integrity of its original lines.

The hotel, church, mills and many other landmarks of Middle Falls have suffered the effects of entropy. The store where Maggie walked to get milk is still standing. It is on the right hand side before the firehouse. The Remington house is the last one, on the left, in the hamlet. It is the one with the long porch. It was next to where Abraham Cipperly heard Maggie's cry. The Cipperly home has been replaced by a car dealership.

The site where Maggie's body

was found is in this short stretch of highway. The body was found to the right (south side) of the highway where the road has been built up. The stone bridge has been removed and the road from Middle Falls to Greenwich straightened and leveled out. The original bridge crossed the creek at almost the same spot as the current bridge (which is really only a covered culvert). It is just before the McDonald's. The upper pond is still visible from the road, but the lower pond, where Maggie's body was found, has since dried up.

Greenwich

is straight ahead on Route 29 east within a mile after route 40 turns left you will be in Greenwich. The location of the church Maggie attended; the homes of the members of the coroner's jury are all noted on the map of Greenwich, as is the home of Mrs. McMaster. These are all within easy walking distance of each other so park your car and walk around. The actual church Maggie attended is now the annex of the Catholic church on Hill Street. Many of the houses and commercial buildings are as Maggie would have known them.

The Greenwich House

managed by Dr. Scott burned in a fire many years ago. It stood at the southeast corner of Main Street and Bridge Street.

The cemeteries

where many of the people who were witnesses are buried was on your left on the way into town. After you have walked around the village take Cottage Street northeast to get to the entrances. There are too many graves to list each here but walk around and see what you can find. The Catholic cemetery, St. Joseph's, is the one on the right side of the road and can be covered in a very short period.

For those who read the book *To Spend Eternity Alone*, the Shermans: Jennie, John and their son Billings are buried near one of the big markers near the top of the hill in Greenwich Cemetery.

Maggie's grave

is near the eastern most entrance in St. Patrick's Cemetery outside Cambridge. The stone is obelisk in shape and stands about five feet tall. To get to St. Patrick's take the road from Greenwich to Cambridge. This is one of those twisting roads that make winter driving such a thrill. After you go through Coila there will be a sign for Center Cambridge, follow the sign. The cemetery is on the right on a slight hill about a mile out of town. Maggie has no headstone but shares the family marker with her mother and brother. To get to Maggie's grave enter through the first entrance. Maggie's resting place is on the left about _ of the way down the short lane.

Fort Edward

has many historical places but many of those that relate to this story are gone. Sites that have disappeared are the Hull house, which stood on the corner of Bridge and Broadway, exactly where the Stewart's store is today. The Eldridge House stood in the area just south of the railroad track on the west side of the road. There is a debate about whether the Waverly House is still at the site. The site is the first building on the north side off the railroad track on Broadway. The lines of the building match the ones in the picture. Some locals maintain the house was moved to the site some time after the deaths. Al Woodin was killed on the tracks between the two buildings. The tracks were raised and the underpass built in 1917. All three of the sites noted above are within a football field from each other. Canal Street where Morgan hanged himself and Hinckley died of consumption runs roughly parallel to Broadway. The homes of Hinckley and Morgan are off East Street. All these homes are again within a very short walk.

The path Page Hull

took on his way to the river was up Broadway to the area near the hill. There he turned and walked toward the old seminary.

The Hull family's graves

and those of all the others from Fort Edward: Morgan, Hinckley and Woodin, are all in the extreme south section of Union Cemetery. Union Cemetery is the large cemetery on Route 4 across from the County Building in Hudson Falls.

When walking these streets I get chills thinking about all the lives wasted in one evening.

**A final note for those readers who felt
that even after reading Maggie's story
they could sleep.**

Publishing a book a year is possible because I only sleep about four or five hours a night. During the course of writing the initial draft of this book I seriously doubt if I ever slept more than two or three hours a night. Although I always feel driven, this story pulled me in with such intensity that the word "driven" took on a whole new meaning.

190

Index of Principal Characters

191